THE IVORY DOOR

A Legend in a Prologue and Three Acts

BY

A. A. MILNE

New York	London	Los Angeles, Calif.
SAMUEL FRENCH	SAMUEL FRENCH, LTD.	SAMUEL FRENCH
Incorporated 1898	26 Southampton St.	Incorporated 1898
25 West 45th Street	Strand, W.C.2	811 West 7th Street

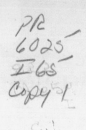

THE IVORY DOOR

Printed in the United States of America

24944

THE IVORY DOOR

A play in three acts by A. A. Milne. Produced by Charles Hopkins at the Charles Hopkins Theatre, New York, October 18, 1927.

CAST OF CHARACTERS

PROLOGUE

KING HILARY	Henry Hull
PRINCE PERIVALE	David Vivian
BRAND	A. P. Kaye

THE PLAY

KING PERIVALE	Henry Hull
BRAND	A. P. Kaye
ANNA	Louise Closser Hale
THORA	Helen Chandler
THE CHANCELLOR	Ernest Lawford
JESSICA	Margaret Gaillard
ANTON	John Pote
OLD BEPPO	Donald Meek
SIMEON	William Boren
COUNT ROLLO	Trevor Bland
THE MUMMER	Edward Nannery
TITUS, SOLDIER OF THE GUARD	Earl McDonald
CARLO, SOLDIER OF THE GUARD	Trevor Bland
BRUNO, CAPTAIN OF THE GUARD	Edward Rigby
PRINCESS LILIA	Linda Watkins

A GLIMPSE INTO THE FUTURE

THE KING	Henry Hull
THE PRINCE	Lawrence Bevans

ACTS I, II AND III. At the King's Castle

Staged by CHARLES HOPKINS.

THE IVORY DOOR

Produced at the Haymarket Theatre, London, W.C., on Wednesday, April the 17th, 1929.

PERSONS OF THE PLAY

PROLOGUE

KING HILARY	Henry Wolston.
PRINCE PERIVALE	Master Harold Reese.
SERVANT	Ernest Ruston.

THE PLAY

KING PERIVALE	Francis Lister.
BRAND (*his* Body-servant)	Frank Allenby.
ANNA	Rosina Filippi.
THORA	Emmie Arthur-Williams.
THE CHANCELLOR	C. M. Lowne.
JESSICA	Joan Harben.
ANTON	Lawrence Ireland.
OLD BEPPO	Wallace Evennett.
SIMEON	Walton Palmer.
COUNT ROLLO	Deering Wells.
THE MUMMER	Tom Reynolds.
TITUS CARLO } (Soldiers of the Guard)	{ Vincent Holman. Henry Wolston.
BRUNO (Captain of the Guard)	Sam Livesey.
PRINCESS LILIA	Angela Baddeley.

A GLIMPSE INTO THE FUTURE

THE KING	Halliday Mason.
THE PRINCE	Master William Salmon.

Play produced by NICHOLAS HANNEN.

5

4

THE IVORY DOOR

PROLOGUE

Once upon a time in the country of—but we need not give it a name. Nor need we say more of the time than that it was " once," long, long ago. Somewhere in the Middle Ages, perhaps, when men were superstitious : but they are superstitious still. Somewhere in France, perhaps—or Germany—or in one of those mysterious countries where the King was little more than King of his Castle ; so that when we have said " Once upon a time there was a King," we have said all that we need to say.

We see the King, good KING HILARY, *seated on his throne, a grave man of middle age. Does he wear his crown ? One feels that he does ; that they always did in those days. Crown or no crown, he is surely the King ; just as surely as this is the Throne Room of his Palace. There are two ways into it—through curtains, one imagines —from the* R. *for those of his people who are to have audience of him, from the* L. *for those who are already within the royal apartments. But there is also a door, a real door this time, hidden at the moment by a tapestry, which leads to—well, we shall see. For it is of this door that we are to tell.*

(When the CURTAIN *is up there is a fanfare of trumpets. Three* HERALDS *are heard announcing, "His Royal Highness Prince Perivale." The first in the distance, the second nearer, the third quite close. Then there is another fanfare.)*

(A SERVANT *comes in from up* L.*)*

SERVANT. His Royal Highness Prince Perivale is without, and begs audience of Your Majesty.

HILARY (*with his foot on stool, his mind elsewhere*). Let him come.

(The SERVANT *withdraws, backing from the royal presence and returns with* PERIVALE.*)*

SERVANT (*raising the curtain*). His Royal Highness Prince Perivale !

(He goes out.)

(We need not stop to describe PERIVALE. *He was only a child at this time—8 or 9 years old. We shall see more of him later.)*

5

PERIVALE. Hallo !
HILARY. Hallo !

(There is a short silence.)

PERIVALE. Do you mind my just coming in and saying "Hallo !"
HILARY. Not when we're alone.
PERIVALE. You see, I'm pretending that (*the* KING *leans forward*) you are King Hilary and I am Prince Perivale, and that I have just come in and—and said "Hallo ! "
HILARY. I see ! (*Rousing himself.*) But as I *am* the King and you're the Prince, and you *have* just come in, we don't need to pretend.
PERIVALE (*with his head on one side*). Why
HILARY. Why, because it is true.
PERIVALE. But you can pretend even if things are true.
HILARY. I don't think I've ever tried doing that. (*Smiling kindly at the little son whom he loves so well.*)
PERIVALE. You see, you pretend that it isn't true (R. *hand out*) so that you can pretend that it *is* (L. *hand out*), so as when you're thinking what a pity it isn't *really*, then you can remember that it's only pretend that it isn't, and it really is. (*Both hands out,* L. *foot up.*)
HILARY. I see.
PERIVALE (*facing front and moving down a step, carelessly*). I think that's a nice way of pretending.
HILARY. It is rather.
PERIVALE (*looking at him*). Why do you say "It is rather" ? It is very.
HILARY. It is very.
PERIVALE (*sighing*). Anna says I'm getting too old to pretend things that aren't true, so that's why I do it the other way round now.
HILARY. As long as you always know the truth in your own mind, Perivale, there's no great harm in pretending.
PERIVALE (*moving up*). There are lots of things to know the truth about, aren't there ? (*Scratching the back of his head.*) The more I seem to know, the more I don't seem to know.
HILARY (*pushing stool towards him*). Well, sit down and see if I know any of them.
PERIVALE (*sitting down on stool*). I like talking to you. You're an understanding sort of man.
HILARY (*laughs*). Am I ?
PERIVALE. Are ordinary fathers nice sort of people, or is it only when they're Kings like you ?
HILARY (*leaning forward*). There must be many fathers who are fond of their children.
PERIVALE (*with a laugh*). Fond isn't being understanding. . . .

(*Turning to* HILARY.)   Do other little boys have to wait until their fathers tell them to sit down ?

HILARY.   It depends.

PERIVALE.   Even *fathers* can't sit down until *you* tell them to, can they ?

HILARY.   No, my son.

PERIVALE (*facing front*).   And nobody *really* can until *I* tell them to—except you, of course.   (*Turning again to him.*)   Can they ?

HILARY.   When you are grown up they will not be able to ; but while you are only a little boy——

PERIVALE.   I shall be King when I'm grown up.

HILARY.   When I am dead, you will.

PERIVALE (*looking at him*).   Oh ! . . .   When *are* you going to be dead, Father ?

HILARY.   I don't know, Perivale.

PERIVALE (*frowning*).   What's it like being dead ?

HILARY.   I don't know that either.

PERIVALE.   Cold, I should think (*facing front*), shouldn't you ?

HILARY.   I wonder.

PERIVALE (*turning to him*).   I thought you knew everything.

HILARY.   Not even our wisest men know about death.

PERIVALE.   But Kings *are* the wisest men, aren't they ?

HILARY.   It is commonly said so.

PERIVALE.   And the handsomest, and the best swordsmen, and the cleverest painters, and the greatest generals, and (*puffing himself out*)—and everything.

HILARY.   It is as well that the people should think so.

PERIVALE (*facing him*).   Shall *I* be when *I* grow up ?

HILARY.   So it will be said.

PERIVALE.   But shan't I be ?

HILARY.   It is almost too much to expect of one man, Perivale.

PERIVALE.   Even if he's the King ?

HILARY.   The more so if he be the King.

PERIVALE.   But ought people to say so if it isn't true ?

HILARY.   You will find that people say many things which are not true ; particularly about Kings.

PERIVALE.   Why ?

HILARY.   Well . . . they do.

PERIVALE.   But why ?

HILARY (*sitting up stiffly*).   You will understand, my son, when you are a man, why these things have to be.

PERIVALE (*smiling and looking up*).   You always say that when you don't want to answer.   Do ordinary fathers say it too ?

HILARY (*with a chuckle*).   I expect so.

PERIVALE (*rising and going to him*).   Will you promise not to say it again to-day ?

HILARY.   I can't promise, Perivale.

PERIVALE.   Oh, *do*, Father !   (*His hands on the arm of throne.*)

HILARY. Well, well, what is it you want to ask me?

PERIVALE (*carelessly, moving away from him*). Nothing particular. Only I don't see how we can ever *really* talk if we keep coming to a stop like that.

HILARY. But I like you to ask me questions. I will explain everything which I can, my dear, my very dear, son. (*With his arm round him.*)

PERIVALE. Well, then, what I want to know is—Do you have to love people *tremendously* before you marry them?

HILARY. Yes, you should.

PERIVALE. Did you love my mother like that?

HILARY. I loved her like that before she died.

PERIVALE. Anna said that you met Mother in the forest before you married her, and you both fell in love with each other, and she thought you were just a student and you thought she was just a peasant, and you loved each other tremendously, and then when the King had to marry the Queen, lo! and behold! they were the ones (*holding out his hands*), and weren't they just surprised and happy, and it's true love which makes the world go on. (*His hands crossed on his shoulders and his head down.*)

HILARY (*with his arm round* PERIVALE'S *neck*). Anna talks too much.

PERIVALE. Did it really happen like that, Father?

HILARY. It is always said to happen like that, my son.

PERIVALE. It's a nice way of happening.

HILARY. That is why people like to think it does happen so.

PERIVALE. But doesn't it?

HILARY (*removing his arm and sitting back*). No, my son. (*Hand on* PERIVALE'S *hand.*) It was arranged that I should marry your mother; and, in accordance with the custom of the country, I met her for the first time on the day that I married her. It will be the same with you.

PERIVALE. Oh! . . . Well, that makes it difficult, because I told Anna I was going to marry *her.*

HILARY (*smiling*). Well, well, we need not think about it yet. There is plenty of time.

PERIVALE. Perhaps I'd better tell her to-night I'm not going to, and then it won't be such a surprise for her afterwards.

HILARY. That will be best.

(*Both nod to each other.*)

PERIVALE (*after a pause, drawing his hand away*). Oh, I knew there was something I really did want to ask you. What does Bruno mean when he says (*imitating* BRUNO'S *voice and gesture*), "By the Ivory Door (HILARY *starts and faces front*) and all the Little Devils, I'll stay here no longer"?

(HILARY *looks sharply at his son, and frowns.*)

HILARY. Who is Bruno ?

PERIVALE (*carelessly*). One of the soldiers.

HILARY. Does he say that ?

PERIVALE. Well, he did this morning. What *is* the Ivory Door, Father ? (*Pointing.*) Is it the little door behind the tapestry there ?

HILARY (*startled, sitting bolt upright*). How did you know there was a door there ?

PERIVALE (*surprised*). Doesn't everybody know ?

HILARY (*muttering*). They talk too much.

PERIVALE (*confidently, leaning towards him*). *I've* known all about it for *hundreds* of years !

HILARY. What do you know ?

PERIVALE (*not so confidently, foot on stool and hand on hip*). That —that you mustn't ask questions about it, and that nobody talks about it, and that perhaps when I'm older, and that—well, perhaps I don't know so *very* much about it. . . . What *is* it, Father ?

(*Music starts.*)

HILARY (*after a pause, rising*). Well (*crossing with* PERIVALE *to up* R.), better that I should tell you than that you should make up a frightening tale for yourself from the chatter of others. (*Lifting him on to the window-seat.*)

PERIVALE. I like *you* telling me. (*He waits eagerly.*)

(HILARY *patting his arms.*)

HILARY (*standing with his hand on his arm*). Your great-grand-father, King Stephen, went through that door on a summer's after-noon, and was never seen again.

PERIVALE (*awed*). Where did he go to ?

HILARY. Nobody knows.

PERIVALE (*looking out of the window*). But where does the door go to ?

HILARY (*taking both his hands*). Nobody knows.

PERIVALE. Why don't they look ?

HILARY. It is said that even to look is death.

PERIVALE. Well, I should want to look just to see if it was.

HILARY. A friend of the King's did. He also was never seen again.

PERIVALE. Has the door always been there ?

HILARY. As long as we have any record.

PERIVALE (*scornfully*). And have only *two* people wanted to see what was behind it ?

HILARY. Alas, no. There are stories of many who have gone through it, and been seen no more. King Stephen was not the first.

PERIVALE. What happens to them ?

HILARY. No one can tell us, for no one has ever come back.

PERIVALE. I wonder what does happen.

HILARY. I used to wonder, Perivale.

PERIVALE (*surprised*). Don't you still ?

HILARY (*moving away to* C.). What does it matter ?

(*Music stops.*)

If the door is never opened, it might as well not be there. (*At throne, facing up stage, hand on arm of throne.*)

PERIVALE (*jumping down*). I expect there's a long dark passage (*pointing up to the Ivory Door*), and then a very deep pit, and in you go—plop !—before you know where you are.

HILARY (*smiling*). It may be so.

PERIVALE. I expect there's a terrible monster just round the corner—waiting for you. Or devils and things. (*Wagging his finger.*)

HILARY. It may be.

PERIVALE (*with arms extended*). I expect you just vanish suddenly, because an old woman snatches you up into the air. (*Clasping his hands.*)

HILARY. All these things may be.

PERIVALE (*with his hand between his knees*). Isn't it exciting ? . . . (*Thoughtfully turning to door.*) Of course if you went through the door you might never come back, but you would know all about it just before you didn't come back. Wouldn't you ?

HILARY. You wouldn't be able to tell anybody. (*Sitting on throne and his* R. *foot on stool.*)

PERIVALE. Of course telling is nice, but knowing is nice too.

HILARY. There are many who believe that they know, and there is none who can gainsay them.

PERIVALE (*going close to the door*). Who has the key, Father ?

HILARY. The key had disappeared before I came to the throne. . . . Nobody knows where it is.

PERIVALE. If you found it, would you go through ?

HILARY (*hesitating, sitting upright*). I—I—— (*Suddenly, with his hands clasping the arms of the throne.*) I would destroy it !

PERIVALE (*looking at him, and dropping his face. Pause*). Perhaps King Stephen's friend took it with him through the door, and it vanished too.

HILARY. It may be.

PERIVALE. Were you alive, Father, when King Stephen was alive ?

HILARY. As a very little boy, yes. I remember him.

PERIVALE. Supposing he had taken you with him, then I should never have been born, should I ?

HILARY (*laughingly*). No, my son.

PERIVALE. What does it feel like, not being born ?

HILARY. I don't know, Perivale.

PERIVALE. Funny, I should think, shouldn't you ? (*Pulling chair to* R. *and placing chair quite close to the front of the door.*) Father ! (*Sitting on chair.*)

HILARY. Yes?

PERIVALE (*sitting facing door, back of chair to it.*) May I just look at it ? (HILARY *hesitates. Then he decides to make light of the matter.*)

HILARY (*cheerfully*). Why not ? (*Picking it up from the bottom, he throws back the tapestry, disclosing the door.*) Just an ordinary door, you see. (*He laughs a little self-consciously.*) Nothing frightening about it.

(PERIVALE *sits on the chair in front of it, pondering it.*)

Nothing to be afraid of, my son, nothing to be afraid of.

PERIVALE (*looking up at his father in sudden surprise*). I wasn't being afraid of it, Father. (*He continues to gaze at it.*) I'm waiting for it to tell me.

Light fades to Black Out.

CURTAIN.

ACT I

SCENE 1

The SCENE *is the same, but it is fifteen years later.* PERIVALE *is King now : the bravest of the brave, the wisest of the wise, and so on. They have been saying it since he came to the throne. If he had not such an ironic sense of humour, he might believe it, for he is a sufficiently decorative-looking King to inspire his people to flattery. But he has a passion for the truth : the truth about himself, which he knows, and the truth about many other matters, of which only he knows that he is ignorant. When we last saw him, he was waiting to know the secret of the Ivory Door. He is still waiting, still wondering. In fact, it is almost within his grasp now, for he has stumbled upon the key to it. As we watch him, we see that he is trying to make up his mind. He walks up and down, glancing always at the door. He takes the key from his pocket, makes to put it in the lock, withdraws and wonders. " Of course you might never come back, but you would know all about it just before you didn't come back "—it was fifteen years ago that he said it, and never since then has that thought been long out of his mind. To know! Wouldn't it be worth anything to know?*

The Throne Room is as we saw it fifteen years ago, save in this one particular ; the tapestry has gone, and we see the Ivory Door. Since it is there, why hide it?

(As the CURTAIN *rises* PERIVALE *is seated up* R. *facing the Ivory Door. He rises, drags chair up, then kneels on chair looking at the Ivory Door. Goes up and puts the key in keyhole, hesitates and moves down* R., *clasping and unclasping his hands. Moving up to door again he unlocks the door, pauses, then moves away again, leaving the key in the lock. Then he goes up and withdraws key and drops it in his pocket.*

PERIVALE *claps his hands, and from an inner apartment up* L. *comes* BRAND, *his body-servant, lean, dark, efficient, faithful to the idea of efficiency, and by reason of his personal sympathy with* PERIVALE'S *ironic humour, rather than from the lofty motives of loyalty and duty such as he would instinctively advance.)*

BRAND (*bowing up* L.C., *then coming* C.). Your Majesty !
PERIVALE (*down* R., *after a pause. Laughs*). I have been King for

12

three years, Brand, and I never get tired of seeing you come in like that.

BRAND. I never get tired of coming in, Your Majesty.

PERIVALE. Excellent! We will humour each other.

(*He waves a hand of dismissal.* BRAND *goes out up* L. PERIVALE *claps his hands again.* BRAND *comes in.*)

BRAND. Your Majesty!

PERIVALE (*throwing out his hands, crossing to window, putting his foot on seat*). There you are!

BRAND (*pause*). Did Your Majesty wish anything?

PERIVALE (*sighing*). A thousand things. . . . But I don't know what they are.

BRAND. Has Your Majesty any commands for me?

PERIVALE (*still looking out*). No commands. (*Kindly.*) A few requests, perhaps.

BRAND (*nobly*). I would die for Your Majesty!

PERIVALE. That was not to be one of them.

BRAND. I am at Your Majesty's service.

PERIVALE. I wonder (*putting his foot down*). . . . Would you go through that door if I asked you? (*He nods towards the Ivory Door.*)

BRAND (*starts back and down a step, then stands at attention, after an anxious glance to make sure that the key is not there*). Yes, Your Majesty, if only it were possible. But there is no key.

PERIVALE (*quietly, crossing to him*). Supposing I were to tell you that I had found the key?

BRAND (*with great fear, cringing and clasping his hands*). Then I would beseech Your Majesty to cast it into the deepest corner of the moat.

PERIVALE (*moving to* R.). And after I had done that?

BRAND (*straightening up*). I should again declare my readiness to go through the door—if only it were possible.

PERIVALE (*moving down and up, shaking his head with a smile*). Your heroism would not deceive me, Brand.

BRAND. It would not be meant to, Your Majesty. It would only be meant to reassure myself. . . . Any other command, Your Majesty?

PERIVALE (*thoughtfully, looking at door*). Tell me, are you really afraid of what is beyond there?

BRAND. One is not afraid of burnt fingers, Your Majesty, but one does not hold one's hand in the flame.

PERIVALE (*down* R.). Death seems to you as certain as that—behind the door?

BRAND (*with a shrug*). We know what has happened to the others.

PERIVALE (*turning to him*). We *don't* know what has happened to the others.

BRAND. It is the same thing, Your Majesty.

PERIVALE (*after a pause, crossing to him*). Supposing *I* were to go through, what would you do ?

BRAND. Give the alarm, Your Majesty.

PERIVALE. And then ?

BRAND. Attach myself to Your Majesty's eldest son.

PERIVALE (*surprised*). My eldest son ?

BRAND. Your Majesty is to wed with the Princess Lilia to-morrow.

PERIVALE. Yes, but—but—— Yes.

BRAND. One has to look ahead, Your Majesty.

PERIVALE. True. (*Moving up and stopping again on the steps of the Ivory Door*). Yet I want to *know*. How can I not *know* ? (*Facing the door.*)

BRAND (*moving up*). We shall know all about death when our time comes, Your Majesty.

PERIVALE. How do we know it is death ? It may be the way into another world.

BRAND. Your Majesty is a King in this one. Would you be better off in another ?

PERIVALE (*turning to him and pointing to door invitingly*). You are a servant in this world—could you be worse off in another ?

BRAND. I might not be servant to so noble a master.

PERIVALE (*nodding with an ironic smile*). Thank you, Brand. You have reassured yourself again.

BRAND. I mean it with all my heart, Your Majesty.

PERIVALE (*crossing to window and looking out, pauses and walks over to throne*). You are a good fellow. . . . (*Quizzically, sitting on throne.*) And so you will look after my eldest son for me ?

BRAND (*portentously*). As I have looked after Your Majesty.

PERIVALE. We must give him a name. What shall we call him ? Perhaps you have already decided ?

BRAND (*shocked*). Your Majesty ! (*With dignity.*) That will be for Your Majesty and the Princess Lilia to decide.

PERIVALE. Ah, I was forgetting the Princess Lilia. She will be there too, of course.

ANNA'S VOICE (*outside, down* R., *archly*). May I come in ?

BRAND (*scandalized*). Your Majesty !

(*He goes quickly towards it, but* ANNA'S *head has already appeared through the curtains. This is that* ANNA *whom* PERIVALE *was pre-pared to marry fifteen years ago : a broad-bodied, loose-minded, irresponsible woman then, who has spread steadily in all these direc-tions with each succeeding year.*)

PERIVALE. You may come in, Anna.

ANNA (*waving* BRAND *who is up* R.C. *on one side with great dignity and crossing to* C.). Of course I may come in. It would be a pretty thing if Old Anna were not allowed to see her boy of a morning.

(*Looking at* BRAND *who replaces chair up* c.)   Who is this young man ?   (*Moving up to* BRAND *and peering at him*.)   I don't think I know this young man.   Young man, you may leave us.

BRAND.   Now, now, Old Anna !

ANNA.   Don't you now-now me !   Who are you to say now-now to me ?

PERIVALE (*helping her on to dais and smiling*).   You may leave us, Brand.

BRAND (*reluctantly*).   Your Majesty—— She is—— (*He touches his head.*)   She knows not how to behave.

ANNA (*indignantly, turning on him*).   Behave !   I not know how to behave !   Why it was I who first taught His Majesty how to behave !   (*With a wink.*)   Aha, I have seen more of His Majesty than you, let me tell you.

PERIVALE (*firmly*).   If you will leave us, Brand, I will see that we both behave.

BRAND.   Your Majesty !

(*He withdraws up* L.C.)

ANNA (*to* PERIVALE *and stroking him soothingly*).   There, there, my darling !   It was lucky I came in when I did, and stopped him being rude to you.   You want your Old Anna to look after you.

PERIVALE.   I want my Old Anna to help me look after somebody else.

ANNA (*nodding*).   Your sweetheart, yes.

PERIVALE (*surprised*).   My sweetheart ?

ANNA.   Your Lilia.

PERIVALE.   Oh ! . . . Yes.

ANNA (*with her arm round his neck*).   Bless you, you don't think Old Anna wouldn't know.

PERIVALE.   I assure you I have no idea what Old Anna knows.

ANNA (*knowingly*).   Old Anna always knows when there's love in the air.

PERIVALE.   I don't understand this talk about love.

ANNA (*chuckling*).   I am sure you don't, Your Majesty.

PERIVALE.   Surely you know that the Princess Lilia and I meet for the first time to-morrow ?

ANNA (*chuckling*).   Oh *I* know !   *I* know !   The first time !   Beautiful !   Beautiful !

PERIVALE (*patiently, but firmly*).   In accordance with the custom of the country, the King's Bride——

ANNA (*chuckling*).   The custom of the country !   Oh, yes, I know all about the custom of the country !   And what harm if they do, *I* say.

PERIVALE (*shaking his head at her*).   Anna !

ANNA.   Oh, I mean no more than kisses, Your Majesty.   Let them wait for more than kisses.   The wedding-night soon comes.

PERIVALE (*firmly*). Have you chosen me the maid for Her Royal Highness ?

ANNA. Yes, Your Majesty, I have her here. Thora. **A** good girl.

PERIVALE. Send her to me. I will see her.

ANNA. Yes, Your Majesty. (*Going to the curtains down* R.) Are you there, dear ?

(THORA *enters, a pretty girl of 18, a little overwhelmed by the sudden glory which has come to her.* ANNA *has crossed to* R. THORA *hiding behind her.* ANNA *turns and finds her.*)

Oh, there you are! You weren't listening, I hope ? Naturally when His Majesty and I get talking together——

PERIVALE. Thank you, Anna.

ANNA (*pushing* THORA *forward, who kneels*). You needn't be afraid of His Majesty, dear. He's a kind man, as I ought to know, having taught him kindness with a slipper.

(PERIVALE *claps his hands.*)

Yes, yes, I'm going, dear. (*She makes her way out as* BRAND *enters and approaches.*) There's that young man again. Who *is* that young man ? I've seen him somewhere. Why don't they push him through the Ivory Door and have done with it ?

(*She goes out, still talking,* BRAND *hurrying her off from behind up* L. *Pause after exit of* BRAND.)

PERIVALE (*to* THORA). So you are to be maid to Her Royal Highness ?

THORA. If it please Your Majesty.

PERIVALE. You will be kind to her ?

THORA. Oh, Your Majesty !

PERIVALE (*rising and standing with one foot on dais*). No, but I mean it. She comes to us a stranger. She comes from her own country to make a home among strangers in a new country. She may bring none of her own people with her beyond the Palace gates. From the moment that she crosses them she is alone with us, a stranger. (*Raising* THORA.) You will be kind to her ?

THORA. Your Majesty, she is to be the Queen !

PERIVALE. All the more reason that she should have a friend in you, Thora.

THORA. She will have Your Majesty.

PERIVALE. True. We must not forget that. (*Sitting on throne.*)

THORA (*smiling, moving up*). Well, there is one old friend for her.

PERIVALE. An *old* friend ?

THORA (*archly*). Oh, Your Majesty, we all know !

PERIVALE. What do you know ? Everybody seems to know things, save myself.

THORA. We know that Your Majesty and Her Royal Highness have been friends, more than friends, these many months.

PERIVALE. Ah yes, I was forgetting that you knew that.

THORA (*above dais*). Oh, Your Majesty, the people always know!

PERIVALE (*dryly*). It appears so. (*Smiling.*) Let me see what they do know. They know that the Princess and I met one day—in the forest?

THORA. Yes, Your Majesty. Accidentally.

PERIVALE. Accidentally. That as soon as we saw each other we were attracted by each other.

THORA. Oh, very much attracted, Your Majesty.

PERIVALE. Very much attracted. That I supposed her to be a simple peasant——

THORA. Yes, Your Majesty.

PERIVALE. Now I wonder why I supposed that?

THORA (*eagerly*). For the reason that she was wearing the dress of a simple peasant.

PERIVALE. That, of course, would account for the mistake. She wore it, I suppose——

THORA. To have more freedom, Your Majesty.

PERIVALE (*nodding*). More freedom.

THORA. Adventures come to the peasant such as never come to the Princess.

PERIVALE. No doubt. Well, then, I was attracted by this simple peasant——

THORA. You had never seen anyone so lovely before!

PERIVALE. Never. In her simple peasant costume she looked particularly beautiful. I was attracted by her, I fell in love with her, and at last I decided to marry her.

THORA (*eagerly*). You feared that you could not.

PERIVALE. I feared that I could not, for that I was a King and she was but a simple peasant.

THORA (*clasping her hands*). Oh, how unhappy you were, Your Majesty!

PERIVALE (*rising*). Miserable. I can hardly bear to think of it even now. . . . Ah, but she loved *me*, Thora! (*Stepping off dais and coming down* R.C.)

THORA (*coming down eagerly*). Yes! Oh, yes! She thought you were the most wonderful man she had ever seen!

PERIVALE (*crossing to* L.). Oh, much the most wonderful! But alas! she feared that she could not marry me, for that she was a Princess, and I, as she supposed, was only a—— Now, what was I?

THORA. A simple huntsman.

PERIVALE (*surprised*). Huntsman? You're sure it was not a student? (*Crossing to* R.) Walking through the forest in strict meditation.

THORA (*smiling*). No, Your Majesty. You see, I *do* know. It was a huntsman, wasn't it?

B

PERIVALE. I shall have to admit that it was, Thora.

THORA. (*nodding eagerly*). You were separated from the hunt; you had fallen; you had struggled through mire and ditch and brake. How could she guess that you were the King?

PERIVALE. How indeed? Yet she fell in love with me.

THORA. Ah, Your Majesty, that is true love! Oh, and think how wonderful for both of you when for the first time you realized the truth!

PERIVALE (*surprised*). The truth? (*Turning away.*) Does *that* come into the story?

THORA (C., *not heeding*). When you realized that the simple peasant whom you loved was the Princess Lilia whom you were pledged to marry; when she knew that the King whose bride she was to be was already her lover. Ah!

PERIVALE (*with a sigh, but not now ironical*). Yes, that would have been—(*he corrects himself*) that was a great moment. (*Crossing to* L.C.) I remember it still.

THORA (*simply*). You will remember it all your life, Your Majesty.

PERIVALE (*at throne*). You are right, Thora.

(THORA *moves up.*)

There should be a moment in the lives of each one of us which we may remember for ever. . . . (*Looking up at the Ivory Door and sitting on throne.*) You love, Thora?

THORA (C., *shyly*). Yes, Your Majesty.

PERIVALE. And are loved in return?

THORA. Yes, Your Majesty.

PERIVALE. Then you will be very kind to the Princess Lilia.

THORA (*simply*). I will be her friend if she will let me.

PERIVALE. Thank you.

(*He holds out his hand. She comes forward to dais.*)

THORA (*a little overcome*). Oh, Your Majesty! (*Kneeling and kissing his hand.*)

PERIVALE (*patting her head*). There's a good girl.

(*He abstractedly dismisses her, clapping his hands.* BRAND *enters from up* L. *coming to* R. *of* THORA, *who goes out*, BRAND *in attendance, up* L.)

BRAND (*re-entering to* C.). His Excellency the Chancellor craves audience, Your Majesty.

PERIVALE (*pondering the door*). I will receive him. (*Crossing to* R.)

(BRAND *goes out up* L. *and returns with the* CHANCELLOR.)

BRAND. His Excellency the Chancellor.

(*He goes out, leaving the* CHANCELLOR—*an elderly, cautious gentleman, to whom all life is something of a political crisis—awaiting His*

Majesty's pleasure. The CHANCELLOR *bows and moves down* L.C.)

PERIVALE (*still looking at the door*). And what does His Excellency think ?

CHANCELLOR (*stepping forward*). On what point, Your Majesty ?

PERIVALE. Let us say the mysterious disappearance of King Stephen.

CHANCELLOR (*shocked, moving a step to* C.). Your Majesty !

PERIVALE (*crossing to him*). What is it ?

CHANCELLOR (*reprovingly*). It is hardly—— That is to say—— Naturally Your Majesty can do no wrong——

PERIVALE (*standing by him, with arms akimbo*). Assume for the moment that he has shocked his Chancellor's feelings. Well ? How ?

CHANCELLOR (*looking hastily at the door and away again*). It is wiser—it is safer, Your Majesty— to avert the eye—*and* the mind —from the—the unknown. I find it so. I find it safer. (*Moving towards dais.*)

PERIVALE (*pointing to door*). Turn the mind on it, and it may no longer be unknown.

CHANCELLOR. So thought your ever-to-be-revered great-grandfather King Stephen the Tenth of blessed but unhappy memory.

PERIVALE (*kindly*). Call him Stephen for the moment. I shall understand.

CHANCELLOR (*with dignity*). What did the death of the ever-to-be-revered King Stephen profit us ? Do we know now ? We do not. If we are not meant to know, Your Majesty, it is the part of a wise man not to inquire. I find it so. I find it safer.

PERIVALE. Yet you must wonder sometimes.

CHANCELLOR. I have little time for wondering.

PERIVALE (*moving to* R.). I have little time for doing anything else.

CHANCELLOR (*after a preparatory cough, coming to* C.). It has occurred to me sometimes, Your Majesty, that I am a man in advance of my time. The thought has occurred to me. I have a philosophy in this matter. The evil spirits who lurk behind the door——

PERIVALE. But that is it. Do they ?

CHANCELLOR. Undoubtedly, Your Majesty. They lurk. But I have this feeling about them. That the less we think about them, the less power they have over us. The less we fear them, the less —the less they frighten us. But, as I say, I am in advance of my time. I do not expect to be followed (*bows*)—save, of course, by Your Majesty, the wisest of the wise.

PERIVALE (*quickly*). I follow you, my dear Chancellor, and I assure you that I am *not* frightened by your lurking devils.

CHANCELLOR. Your Majesty frightened ! The bravest of the brave ! Could I have said it ! But may I humbly represent to

Your Majesty that in my philosophy to—er—defy these evil spirits
is of a piece with fearing them. I have this feeling : the less we
defy them, the less they resent our defiance. To ignore them, that
is the only true philosophy. I find it so. I find it safest.

PERIVALE (*crossing to him and looking at him with a smile*). You
have a curious way of ignoring them. (*Crossing to throne and
sitting.*) Well, well ! And now, what is it, Your Excellency ?

CHANCELLOR. Your Majesty, Her Royal Highness the Princess
Lilia's Messenger, Count Rollo, is arrived and craves audience.

PERIVALE. I will see him.

CHANCELLOR (*hesitatingly*). Your Majesty——

PERIVALE. Well ?

CHANCELLOR. If I have Your Majesty's permission to put my
thoughts into words ?

PERIVALE. Into a limited number of words.

CHANCELLOR. There is a certain ceremony in these matters. In
presenting to Your Majesty Her Royal Highness' marriage-gift,
the young Count Rollo will assuredly desire to make a speech.

PERIVALE. I will assuredly listen to it. (*Sitting back on throne
with his eyes shut.*)

CHANCELLOR. It is most gracious of Your Majesty. (*He hesitates.*) H'r'm'——

PERIVALE. Well ?

CHANCELLOR. Your Majesty, without doubt the speech, as pre-
pared by the young Count Rollo, will fall into periods, such as are
most naturally ended by bursts of applause or laughter.

PERIVALE. I will applaud—and laugh.

CHANCELLOR. Your Majesty is ever generous. My only thought
was that, if the ceremony were made public—a select few—one could
arrange for the applause and laughter without taxing Your Majesty's
generosity. It has often been done. It is found safer. Believe
me, Your Majesty, the people are readily moved to enthusiasm over
anything which concerns Your Majesty.

PERIVALE. How kind of them. Let them attend, such as wish
it.

CHANCELLOR. Your Majesty, they will esteem the privilege
beyond all words of mine. Your Majesty's forthcoming marriage
has appealed in an unprecedented way to the imagination of the
people. (*Slyly.*) The—romance of it, if I may say so unofficially,
Your Majesty.

PERIVALE (*ironically*). My dear Chancellor, it is indeed a romance.
I meet her for the first time to-morrow.

CHANCELLOR (*with a nod*). Officially, Your Majesty. But, if I
may so unofficially—— (*He hums roguishly.*)

PERIVALE. So it seems.

CHANCELLOR (*enthusiastically*). An alliance between the most
beautiful lady (as I am assured, and as Your Majesty needs no
telling)—the most beautiful lady in the world, and the wisest

philosopher, the most brilliant swordsman and the most gifted and endowed monarch of the time.

PERIVALE. It becomes more romantic every minute.

CHANCELLOR. Then I have Your Majesty's permission to proceed with the matter ?

PERIVALE. As you will.

CHANCELLOR (*retiring, moving down* L.). Thank you, Your Majesty.

PERIVALE (*as the* CHANCELLOR *is vanishing down* L.). Your Excellency !

CHANCELLOR (*hastily appearing again*). Your Majesty !

PERIVALE (*thoughtfully*). What did happen to King Stephen ?

CHANCELLOR (*shocked*). No, no, Your Majesty ! Let us ignore ! Let us ignore ! I implore Your Majesty ! I find it safer !

(PERIVALE *laughs and gives him a nod of dismissal, and the* CHANCELLOR *goes out by opening down* L. PERIVALE *claps his hands and* BRAND *comes in from up* L.)

BRAND (C.). Your Majesty !

PERIVALE. Am I well dressed enough to receive a gentleman who is to make a long speech ?

BRAND. No, Your Majesty.

PERIVALE (*with a sigh*). I was afraid not. Well, let us see what we can do. (BRAND *draws back the curtains* R. *leading to the private part of the Palace. As he moves to it,* PERIVALE *says :*) I am the greatest philosopher and the most brilliant swordsman in the country. Did you know that, Brand ?

BRAND (*surprised*). But all the country knows that, Your Majesty.

PERIVALE (*nodding*). They all know things—save me. (*Looks at the Ivory Door.*) I am the only ignorant man.

(*He goes out door up* L. BRAND *shrugs his shoulders and follows him.*)

(*The sightseers drift in, a mixed crowd, from door* R. ANTON *is a very superior young man, albeit that he is condescending to marry* JESSICA, *a young woman of inferior manners and intelligence.* ANTON *is always a step or two ahead of her, pretending that she belongs to somebody else : she is always hurrying after him : thus they go through life.* OLD BEPPO *makes no claim on our attention, nor wishes to, save by reason of his age ; he might have been dead and is not.* SIMEON *is a man of ideas. In any company he would say something, and tell his wife afterwards what he said.*)

JESSICA (L.C.). Anton ! Anton ! Is that the Ivory Door ?

ANTON (L.C.). The Ivory Door ? (*To* R. *of her.*) Oh, yes, yes, that will be it, no doubt.

SOME OF THE OTHERS (*to each other*). That's the Ivory Door !

JESSICA (*coming below* ANTON). Grandfather used to tell us about it when we were children. He was alive when the King went through it !

THE OTHERS. Her grandfather went through it ! (*They turn and creep a step towards the Ivory Door.*)

ANTON (*moving up to front of crowd*). Stephen ? Yes, yes, your grandfather would have been alive then.

JESSICA. Grandfather said that the Devil was waiting for King Stephen and changed him into a Black Leopard. He waits behind the door, Grandfather said, and changes anybody who goes through into a Black Leopard.

ANTON. A Black Leopard, yes. That's what happens to anybody who goes through the Ivory Door. He's changed into a Black Leopard.

JESSICA (*to the others*). My grandfather used to tell me. You see he was alive when King Stephen was alive. That's how he knew.

BEPPO (*pushing his way forward through the crowd*). Who was alive when King Stephen was alive ? Show him to Old Beppo, and let him say it to Old Beppo's face.

THE OTHERS. Her grandfather was.

ANTON (*condescendingly*). The child's grandfather.

BEPPO (C.). Her grandfather. Well, show me her grandfather, if he *is* her grandfather.

JESSICA (*forward a step*). Oh, but he's dead now !

BEPPO. What did I tell you ? He knew he couldn't look me in the face and say he was alive. Why ? Because *I'm* the only man in the country who *was* alive and *is* alive.

SIMEON (*eagerly*). Then *you* can remember when the Devil changed the King into a Black Leopard ?

BEPPO. Who says he was changed into a Black Leopard ?

ANTON (*leaning towards him*). An idle story of the girl's grandfather. (*Moving towards throne.*)

BEPPO (*crossing to him*). Show me her grandfather. Let him say it to my face.

SIMEON. Isn't it true ?

ALL (*closing in*). What did happen ? What did happen ?

BEPPO. What did happen ? Ah ! The story went about that he was carried off by the Devil on his Black Horse ; and some say that on still moonless nights you can hear them going Home together— *cloppity, cloppity, cloppity*—him and the Devil riding Home together on his great Black Horse. . . . (*In a whisper, going down on his haunches.*) *Cloppity—cloppity—cloppity.* . . .

(JESSICA *backs to* L.)

(*There are shudders in his audience.*)

ANTON (*carelessly*). Yes, I heard that.

BEPPO (*right up to him, face up, firmly*). You heard it, but it isn't true.

ANTON (*unmoved*). So I always understood. (*Falling back a step.*)

BEPPO. How do I know? Because I was alive and these things were revealed unto me. Stephen fell into the Bottomless Pit (*all heads lowered*) same as all the others did, same as they always will, if they go a-venturing through the Ivory Door. (*All fall back.*)

ANTON (*crossing to* L. *to the others*). That was how it was. The Bottomless Pit.

(*Murmurs from* CROWD.)

JESSICA (*stubbornly*). Well, my grandfather said——

THE OTHERS (*laughing*). Her grandfather!

JESSICA (*whimpering to herself as she returns to the back of the crowd*). My grandfather said—(*sniff*)—Black Leopard—(*sniff*)—I always thought—(*sniff—crossing to* L. *of* ANTON)—Black Leopard—I still think—(*sniff*)—Black Leopard—— (*She dissolves into tears.*)

(ANTON *crosses* C.)

SIMEON. Now tell me, Old Beppo; if common folk like you or me went through that door—would the Devil trouble about common folk like you or me? Or is it only the great and glorious he lies in wait for?

BEPPO (*testily*). Didn't I tell you there was a Bottomless Pit awaiting for all?

ANTON (*to* L. *of* BEPPO). Precisely.

SIMEON. I just asked the question. (*Sticking to it.*) Well, now, someone from afar, the Princess Lilia, as it might be, would the Devil's works have power over *her*, coming from afar? Might it not be that his power, being as you would say——

ANTON. Local. Exactly. Local. It may be, it may be.

BEPPO (*surveying* ANTON *contemptuously*). If this old, old grandfather man I see before me were alive when King Stephen was alive, let *him* tell you. I know nothing. I'm only a baby.

(*Fanfare of trumpets.*)

SIMEON. Come, come, nothing was meant——

BEPPO (*in weak anger*). Let him say it to my face. Let him say it man to man. Let him——

ALL. H'sh!

(*The* CHANCELLOR *comes in from down* L., *commanding silence with a gesture. A servant or two takes up position. Then from up* L. *comes* PERIVALE, *kingly dressed,* BRAND *in attendance, and we all prostrate ourselves.* PERIVALE, *with a kindly nod to us, seats himself on the throne.*)

PERIVALE (*to the* CHANCELLOR). We will receive Count Rollo.

CHANCELLOR. Your Majesty!

(Second fanfare of trumpets.)

(ANTON *moves* R.   JESSICA *runs to him.)*

(All kneel.)

(He makes a sign, and COUNT ROLLO *is ushered in, followed by two attendants carrying a picture wrapped up in an embroidered cloth. We see at once that* ROLLO *is delighted with himself and his clothes. The only thing he is not quite sure of is his speech. However, Beauty is often inarticulate.)*

(Third fanfare of trumpets.)

(Crowd move down R.)

Count Rollo !

PERIVALE *(holding out his hand)*.   I am well pleased to see you, Count.

ROLLO *(coming to dais and kissing* PERIVALE'S *hand, standing)*. Your Majesty is most gracious.

(But you feel that it is really ROLLO *who is being gracious.)*

PERIVALE.   You come from the Princess Lilia ?

ROLLO.   Charged with her duty to Your Majesty, and a humble gift for Your Majesty's acceptance.

PERIVALE.   It is a gift which I shall treasure.

ROLLO *(giving his hat to* BRAND*)*.   Your Majesty—*(he clears his throat)*—this privilege which has fallen upon me—this privilege—I am privileged—*(making a new start)*—Your Majesty, I am deeply sensible of the *(pause)* privilege—coming as I do, as I am privileged to do, on behalf of that noble lady, Her Royal Highness the Princess Lilia—

(The CHANCELLOR *leads cheers with a gesture, then loud cheers from all, during which* ROLLO *glances at his notes, and ends his period.)*

—Her Royal Highness the Princess Lilia. *(A few cheers, led by the* CHANCELLOR.*)*   She, as yet, is a stranger to Your Majesty's people ; the fame of Your Majesty, on the other hand, is known not only to his own people, but to the peoples of all the world. *(Loud cheers.)* We have a saying in our country—" Do not blame the hawk because it cannot sing " *(*CHANCELLOR *and populace laugh)*—by which we mean that to no man is given all the virtues *(laughter)*.   To no man save Your Majesty *(cheers)*.   As statesman *(cheers)*, as orator *(cheers)*, as general *(cheers)*, as swordsman *(cheers)*, as philosopher and poet *(cheers)*, Your Majesty is—not only to his own people, but to the peoples of all the world—*(his voice goes up, as if he hoped for much more from the sentence, but finding nothing, he takes his voice down and finishes it)*—to the peoples of all the world *(cheers)*.   Your Majesty, I am charged with the proud duty of presenting to Your Majesty from the Princess Lilia a gift which, if I may venture to say

so, will ot all gifts be most acceptable to Your Majesty—a present-
ment, a portrait by the hand of our Court painter——

CHANCELLOR (*with admiration*). Ah!

(*Pause.*)

ROLLO. A portrait of Her Royal Highness herself. (*Servants
move, but* ROLLO *stops them.*)

CHANCELLOR. A beautiful thought!

ROLLO. Your Majesty is himself a painter—(PERIVALE's *eye-
brows go up, and the people cheer*)—and, as such, will be able to judge
of the skill of the artist, no less than, as a man, of the beauty of
the woman. (*The picture is brought forward.*) Your Majesty, I have
the honour, on behalf of my mistress the Princess Lilia, to present
this humble gift to Your Majesty. (*To the* CHANCELLOR *under his
breath.*) Is that all right?

CHANCELLOR. Splendid!

(*He withdraws a pace.* ROLLO *removes the cover, which* BRAND *takes
from him and off. The picture is displayed, and the court expresses
its admiration of* LILIA's *cold beauty.*)

PERIVALE (*rising*). Count Rollo, I thank you heartily for the
courteous way in which you have discharged your duty. You are
right in supposing that I could desire no more gracious gift. My
gratitude to the lady, your mistress, who has sent it, I will render
to-morrow.

(*Holding out his hand to* ROLLO.)

ROLLO. At your service, Your Majesty. (*Kisses hand.*)

PERIVALE (*to the* CHANCELLOR). Your Excellency will charge
himself with the entertainment of this gentleman for as long as he
cares to remain our guest.

CHANCELLOR (*pause—awkwardly*). In accordance with custom,
Your Majesty——

PERIVALE. I was forgetting. (*To* ROLLO.) You return at
once?

ROLLO. With Your Majesty's permission.

PERIVALE. Good fortune attend you! . . . Brand!

(BRAND *comes down to* L. *of the picture.*)

ROLLO. And Your Majesties! (*Moving back.*)

(*He bows and goes out.* BRAND *takes the picture from his attendants
and they follow him. Fanfare of trumpets on exit of* CHANCELLOR.
The CHANCELLOR *turns, bows to* PERIVALE, *and follows them. The
crowd cheer and back out after the* CHANCELLOR. *The cheering dies
away in the distance.*)

PERIVALE. Put it there, Brand, and leave me.

(BRAND *places the picture on a chair up* c. *and goes out by opening up* L.)

(*Removing his cloak and turning up to the picture*). We meet at last. (*Studying it closely.*) Cold, proud, beautiful. How would you have looked in peasant dress ? (*Moving back to* c.) Still cold, still proud, still beautiful. (*He looks at the Ivory Door and shrugs his shoulders.*) *You* will not grieve for *me*.

(*The lights fade out.*)

CURTAIN.

SCENE 2

(*It is early next morning. The Throne Room is in darkness, the curtains still drawn. From up* L. BRAND *enters, carrying a lantern.* PERIVALE *follows him.*)

PERIVALE (*moving up to* c. *to* R.). Pull the curtains, Brand.

(BRAND *draws them back, and the early morning sunlight streams into the room.*)

Morning. (*Facing the window.*) My last—or my first ?

BRAND (*putting down the lantern and coming to him*). Your Majesty ! Don't !

PERIVALE (*crossing to window*). Ah, but I must.

BRAND (c. *to* L. *up stage*). Your Majesty may not believe——

PERIVALE. I believe nothing.

BRAND. You may scoff at the tales you hear—sorceries, enchant-ments, devils——

PERIVALE. I scoff at nothing.

BRAND. Then, Your Majesty——

PERIVALE. I am just an ignorant man. I want to know.

BRAND (*backing to door up* L., *boldly*). An inquisitive man.

PERIVALE (R. *of the Ivory Door*). On this point, yes. That door has been with me too long, Brand. It was in my dreams as a child, night and day. I have imagined terrible things of it, I have ima-gined beautiful things. Now I shall know whether it is terrible, or beautiful (*standing on step*) or—nothing.

BRAND. The others never came back.

PERIVALE. Now I shall know why.

BRAND (*coming forward and kneeling—urgently*). Your Majesty, Your Majesty, the door may lead here or there, all that they tell of it may be folly—but this we do know, this is not folly. The others never came back.

PERIVALE (*with a smile*). Then *I* shall never come back.

(BRAND *rises and retreats to* L.)

(*Whimsically to himself, turning.*) I wonder why.

BRAND (*regarding him steadily*). Your Majesty is a brave man.

PERIVALE (*coming to* BRAND *up* C., *who kneels. Ironically*). The bravest of the brave!—how often has it been recited. In truth, I am only a little obstinate. To be frank, Brand, that door offends me. When I come back, if I come back, we will all walk through it in a company (*his hand on* BRAND'S *head*), singing songs of derision (*holding his* R. *hand up*).

BRAND (*muttering*). It is not a subject for jest.

PERIVALE. Not yet. But it may be. . . . Give me the lantern. (*He takes the key from his pocket, moving down* R.)

BRAND (*taking up lantern*). To-day of all days! Your marriage-day!

PERIVALE. The last day on which I am responsible only to myself. To-day I am Perivale—to-morrow I shall be—(*he shrugs his shoulders*)—somebody's husband.

BRAND. To-day you are King Perivale.

PERIVALE (*crossing to* BRAND). But there is always a King. I leave no eldest son for you, Brand, but there is a cousin . . . and you can give the alarm.

BRAND (*pulling himself together bravely*). I—I will come with Your Majesty.

PERIVALE. No, no. The Princess Lilia may need you. You must think of some story—that I did it for her sake—I know not how, but for her sake—it was her life or mine—a story that will go well to music, that mothers can sing to their children.

BRAND (*dully*). I do not understand, Your Majesty.

PERIVALE. There is no need to. (*Taking the lantern, and moving to* R.) Give me—how long shall we say?—three hours. Until then I am in bed. If in three hours from now I do not know everything, I shall never know . . . and you can give the alarm. (*Moving up* C.)

BRAND (*catching hold of* PERIVALE'S *arm in a last effort to stop him*). Your Majesty!

PERIVALE (*violently*). You fool! I must have the truth! (BRAND *cowers back to* L.) May a King never have the truth? (*Gently.*) Put out your hand. (BRAND *holds his hand out wonderingly.*) Farewell. (*He kisses* BRAND'S *hand formally. Then with a smile he says :*) That, at least, is as true as the other way round. (*Briskly, going up to door.*) Now, Brand, I must be alone. (*He puts the key to the lock.*) Else some of your devils may be popping out at you.

BRAND (*shiveringly*). Farewell, Your Majesty.

(PERIVALE *watches him as he disappears through the curtains up* L. *Then he unlocks the door, and puts the key back in his pocket. The door swings slowly open. Involuntarily he starts back ; then, getting control of himself, walks firmly through. The door swings slowly after him—then, with a clang, shuts itself.* BRAND, *his head through the curtains, is watching, terrified, as the door is closing.*)

CURTAIN.

ACT II

Scene 1

Beneath the outer walls of the Castle. It is two hours since we last saw
PERIVALE, *and in that time he has discovered the secret of the Ivory*
Door. Now he comes back to us: dusty, torn and dishevelled from
much stumbling along a dark and narrow passage, but safe in the
sunlight again.

PERIVALE (*entering from* R.). So that was all! Another legend.
. . . We talk the truth out of everything.

(*He sits down on the bank beneath the wall* L. *of* C. *From the* L. *the*
MUMMER *comes into the scene. We hear him first, carolling blithely*
to himself; not because he is particularly happy, but because for the
moment—early in the morning of a summer's day—he sees himself
as a carefree vagabond, enjoying the early summer morning. But
he will play any part you like, and, at 50 or so, he has had a good
deal of experience.)

MUMMER (*crossing to* C.). Ha! Company!
PERIVALE. Do you object to company?
MUMMER. On the contrary, friend, I welcome company. I
expand to company. Such is my nature.
PERIVALE. You are welcome to expand in *my* company, if you
wish it.
MUMMER (*sitting down and placing his bundle on ground on the*
R. *of* PERIVALE). I accept your invitation, friend. . . . I am for
the Castle.
PERIVALE. I wish you joy of it.
MUMMER. And you?
PERIVALE. Presently. (*Hand to his chin.*)

(*The* MUMMER *unpacks his breakfast.*)

MUMMER (*humming, then looking up at* PERIVALE). You are
thoughtful. You have come from far?
PERIVALE. A long and dusty way, with disillusion at the end
of it. I meditate on Disillusion.
MUMMER. Fortunately life gives us many opportunities of so
meditating. But one always comes back to realities. Food is the
great reality. You will share my breakfast?

28

PERIVALE. Thankfully. (*He accepts his share.*) For fifteen years I have dreamed, I have wondered, I have imagined. To-day I have discovered the truth.

MUMMER (*with his mouth full, passing the bottle*). Then is the moment to drink.

PERIVALE (*taking it*). I thank you. (*He drinks.*)

MUMMER. And the truth is——?

PERIVALE. Nothing.

MUMMER. Neither good nor bad? (*Keeping his eye on the bottle.*)

PERIVALE. Neither good nor bad. Just nothing. (*Drinking again.*)

MUMMER (*recovering the bottle*). Your need is not so great as I had feared. One must welcome the good—thus. (*He drinks.*) One must console oneself for the bad—thus. (*He drinks.*) But if it be neither good nor bad, one drinks but for the sake of drinking —thus. (*He drinks.*)

PERIVALE. I am glad to know the philosophy of it.

MUMMER. Of Food I have no philosophy, save that her hand-maiden, Sleep, is ever in attendance. I eat, I sleep; I wake, I drink. This morning I must be wakeful, for I have business at the Castle. The food, therefore, is yours, friend. (*Putting bundle on* PERIVALE'S *knee.*) I confine myself to the bottle. (*Holding up the bottle, and drinking.*) And what might you be by profession who seek the truth so earnestly?

PERIVALE. I? Oh, nothing very much—I am a King.

MUMMER (*laughing*). That's good! That's very good!

PERIVALE. I am glad you like it.

MUMMER. A King! Do you know what I am?

PERIVALE. You have travelled, at least. So much I can see.

MUMMER. Travelled, ay! How could I be here an I had not travelled? For behold! I am the Emperor of China! (*Sitting with feet up and arms folded.*)

PERIVALE (*bowing to him*). Your Imperial Majesty is welcome in my country.

MUMMER. It isn't often, I dare say, that an Emperor and a King sit down to their bit of breakfast together.

PERIVALE. Fortunately not, for I confess that I have always found it fatiguing.

MUMMER (*clapping him on the back.* PERIVALE *is a little surprised*). Capital! You show promise—on my soul you do!

PERIVALE. Promise of what?

MUMMER (*whispering*). You should be in my profession.

PERIVALE (*whispering*). I understood that I was.

MUMMER. Now, now, let us be serious!

PERIVALE. I cannot be more serious, I promise you.

MUMMER. I put it to you. If I am not the Emperor of China, what am I?

PERIVALE. The Empress. Is it a riddle?

MUMMER. Not that I would change places with the Emperor, mark you, for I will have nothing said against my profession.

PERIVALE. It is a better profession than the Emperor's, I make no doubt.

MUMMER (*proudly*). I am a mummer!

PERIVALE (*with a shrug*). Ah, well, it's the same.

MUMMER. Now if you had gone to one of the countryfolk around here, and said boldly as you said to me, " I am the King! " it may be that he would have believed you.

PERIVALE. I think perhaps that he would.

MUMMER. But when you say it to me, I don't believe you. Why?

PERIVALE. I have no idea.

MUMMER. Why, because I am familiar with Kings. I have played a hundred Kings. I know how Kings talk.

PERIVALE. How do they talk? I have often wondered.

MUMMER. It is not so much what they say, as how they say it. It is not so much how they say it, as how they look it. It is not so much how they look it, as how they feel it. (*Rising.*) It is an art. (*Sitting again.*) There is a kingly air and a common air.

PERIVALE. Mine was the common air. I felt it.

MUMMER. Ah, well, you lack the practice. But I could make something of you. (*Rising.*) Now suppose that I am giving one of my renowned and popular renderings of the Emperor of China. How do I play it?

PERIVALE. I am hoping to see.

MUMMER (*rising, with a wave of the hand*). These are my castle walls. I saunter by the side of them, deep in kingly thought. (*He saunters, sheathes dagger and shades eye with his hand.*) I espy you here (*he espies*) where you have no business to be. I bid you begone. That, in the rough, is the situation; the bones of the play. Now then! Mark me! (*He goes out and comes in.*) I approach terribly. (*He goes out and does it again—more terribly.*) Approaches terribly. Espies (*action.*) Says commandingly—now mark this—What have we here?

PERIVALE (*meekly*). Me. What do I say?

MUMMER. Let me think! . . . Yes, this will give it to me: Tremblingly—" A poor man, Your Majesty, who means no harm."

PERIVALE (*tremblingly*). A poor man, Your Majesty, who means no harm.

MUMMER. Excellent! Excellent! The common touch—you have it. It comes natural to you. (*Murmuring to himself.*) A poor man, Your Majesty—now just give me that again. What——

PERIVALE. A poor man——

MUMMER. Wait for it! (*Commandingly, stamping his foot*). What have we here?

PERIVALE. A poor man, Your Majesty, who means no harm.

MUMMER (*terribly*). Begone to thy kennel, thou rascally rogue, ere I set my dogs on thee!

PERIVALE. Yes, I should be gone in that case.

MUMMER. You see! The royal touch. One has it or one has not. There is no mistaking it. Now let me see what *you* make of it.

(PERIVALE *rises*.)

Goes out left.

(PERIVALE *crosses to* L.)

Enters terribly. Discovers varlet against Castle wall. Dismisses varlet.

(*Exit* PERIVALE.)

Now then. (*He assumes character of varlet and sits.*)

PERIVALE (*entering terribly*). What——

MUMMER. Good! Good! A little more air.

PERIVALE (*moving back and re-entering*). What have we here!

MUMMER. A poor man, Your Majesty, who means no harm.

PERIVALE (*foot on stone, drawing dagger quietly*). Get thee hence, thou pock-faced knave, else I cleave thee to the marrow! (*Holding up dagger.*)

MUMMER. Er—promising: very promising. But just lacking in that something. You see the difference? The kingly air, the common air. There is no mistaking it.

PERIVALE (*with a yawn*). Well, if I lack the kingly air, I must needs make my way without it. (*Crossing* R.C.)

MUMMER. You are off?

PERIVALE (*lazily*). I should be homewards, for they will be looking for me, but it is pleasant here.

MUMMER. You have a home? I took you for a wanderer like myself.

PERIVALE. A sort of home. (*He sits down again on the ground* R. *of stone.*) Yet, in a way, hardly a home.

MUMMER. You are married, perhaps? I had sworn to you for a single man.

PERIVALE. To be frank, friend, I am to be married to-day.

MUMMER (*gloomily*). I wish you well.

PERIVALE. I thank you for your enthusiasm.

MUMMER. Is she beautiful? (*Tying up his bundle.*)

PERIVALE. They say so. I have never seen her.

MUMMER. Beware of beautiful women.

PERIVALE. I will remember your warning.

MUMMER. Does she speak with a fair, soft voice?

PERIVALE. So they tell me. I have never spoken with her.

MUMMER. Be very ware of the fair, soft voice.

PERIVALE (*smiling*). I will mistrust its every word.

MUMMER. Has she a firm, cool hand?

PERIVALE. They credit her with it. I have never touched it.

MUMMER. Misdoubt the firm, cool hand.

PERIVALE. I will suspect the worst of it.

MUMMER (*surprised, looking at him*). How comes it that you marry a woman whose face you have never seen, whose voice you have never heard, whose hand you have never touched?

PERIVALE (*lightly*). It is the way in our family.

MUMMER. Perhaps it is as good a way as another. There can be no recriminations between you afterwards.

PERIVALE. I perceive that you are an enthusiast about marriage.

MUMMER. No, I am not an enthusiast.

PERIVALE (*apologetically*). Your pardon. I mistook you.

MUMMER. But I wish you well. (*He takes a last drink.*)

PERIVALE (*looking at him*). I am glad of your good wishes. Let us hope that they will avail me.

MUMMER. Well, I am for the Castle.

PERIVALE. Fare you well.

MUMMER (*going* R., *humming*). Farewell.

(*The* MUMMER *sings to himself. He stops, looks back at* PERIVALE, *says scornfully,* "A King!", *laughs, and goes on with his song and his journey. Exit to* L.)

CURTAIN.

SCENE 2

The Courtyard of the Castle. At the back is the Great Gate through which the PRINCESS LILIA *must come to her bridegroom—almost at any moment now. On the* R., *steps lead up to the entrance to the Palace; on the* L. *are the soldiers' quarters.*

Two of the soldiers, CARLO *and* TITUS, *are on guard, or would be if they thought their* CAPTAIN *was at hand.* CARLO, *in fact, is finishing off a late night's sleep, on bench up* L.C., *while* TITUS *marches idly up and down thinking of the girl he is going to marry. A mile away the* MUMMER *has said* "Farewell" *to* PERIVALE *and is climbing the hill.*

(TITUS, *pacing from* R. *to* L. *and to* C., *catches sight of* CARLO *suddenly, attracted by his snores, and decides to indulge the sense of humour which his girl admires so much in him. He tiptoes to a position at the top of the Palace steps down* R.)

TITUS (*in a loud official voice*). His Majesty King Perivale!

(CARLO *wakes up with a start, and jumps to his feet, picking up spear.* TITUS *roars with laughter.*)

CARLO (*sulkily*). A fool's trick. (*Putting spear down again.*)

TITUS. You'd have looked the fool if it had truly been His Majesty. (*Coming down from steps and going up* R.)

CARLO. I'm not afraid of any Majesty. (*Sitting down* L.)

TITUS (*ironically*). I had noticed it, Carlo.

CARLO. Not man to man. (*Yawning.*) I would fight him, if he would fight man to man. (*Yawning again.*)

TITUS. You! (*Moving towards him at* C.) He could pass the time with three of you together, and then not be properly breathed for his wedding. (*Leaning on* L. *side of gate* C.) Did you never hear how he dealt with the Five Robbers in the Forest? He was riding alone, going to meet the Princess Lilia, they say, when suddenly——

CARLO (*growling*). They say! They say many things. This Princess Lilia that we wait for now——

TITUS (*ironically*). So alertly——

CARLO (*quickly*). Time enough when the Great Bell sounds. This Princess Lilia, our new Queen, rest our souls, do you know what they say of *her*?

TITUS (*smilingly*). That she is the most beautiful woman in the world.

CARLO. And so she may be. And so, seeing where she comes from, I make no doubt she is.

TITUS (*surprised*). Where she comes from?

CARLO (*nodding*). They say she's the Devil's Brat. They say her mother——

TITUS (*turning to him*). Who says it?

CARLO. Who says it? Everyone says it. It is well known.

TITUS (*annoyed*). *I* don't know it.

CARLO. That's why I'm telling you. Her mother was in league with the Devil. All women are, as far as that goes, but she went further than most. One night, so they say, when her husband the King——

TITUS (*contemptuously, walking away to* R.). Keep your silly lies for your friends in the tavern. I'll have none of them.

CARLO (*rising and going to him*). Lies, you say. I'll prove it to you. (*Weightily.*) Now then. If she is the Devil's Brat, what would you expect her to have? You would expect her to have pointed ears.

TITUS (*slowly*). Why?

CARLO (*annoyed*). Why? Because that's how you recognize them, of course.

TITUS (*reluctantly*). Well?

CARLO. Well, if she had pointed ears, what would you expect her to do? You would expect her to hide them, being the Devil's Brat and up to the Devil's tricks to deceive saintly men.

TITUS. Well?

CARLO. Well, your Princess Lilia *does* hide them! She wears her hair low down on her head so as to hide her ears from saintly

C

men. (*With conviction.*) The Devil's Brat. (*Spits and moves to* L.C.)

TITUS (*impressed*). Ah !

CARLO. And if you ask *me* what is on the other side of the Ivory Door, I can tell you that too. (*Coming to* C., *impressively.*) Her uncles and her aunts and her cousins and her nephews, and all the whole tribe of them—waiting for King Perivale ! (*Sitting on stool* R. *of table* L.)

TITUS (*uneasily*). Lies !

CARLO. Facts. There's no running away from facts. Mind you (*picking his teeth and leaning on table*), I say nothing against the King getting married. From all I hear it's time he *was* married. (*Chuckles.*) Everybody knows——

TITUS (*furiously approaching him with spear down*). Say another word against the King, and I'll run you through where you sit.

CARLO. Easy friend, easy ! (*Pushing spear-head away.*)

TITUS (*again threatening him*). I warn you I'll hear nothing against His Majesty. As proper a king——

CARLO (*shaking his head sadly. Rising and pushing the spear-head up perpendicularly*). You're a simple fellow, Titus. I know your sort. One of those simpletons who believe the best of everybody.

TITUS. And I know *your* sort. One of those innocents who believe the worst of everybody. And your sort of fool is the bigger fool of the two.

CARLO (*pulling at his dagger*). Innocent !

(TITUS *moves to* R.)

(*Aghast.*) You dare to call me innocent ! No man calls me innocent and lives.

TITUS (*laughing*). I have already called you a liar, and I live.

CARLO (*furiously*). I care nothing for your liar. But innocent ! (*Crossing up* L.) Spear or dagger, which you will. I'll have your blood for that word.

TITUS (*putting down his spear and taking out his dagger*). Dagger. then. (*With mock fear dancing to* L., CARLO *crossing to* R.) But if I die, Carlo, if you kill me, Carlo, will you do one thing for me, Carlo ?

CARLO. Well ?

TITUS. Tell my friends that I died—believing in your innocence ! (*He laughs.*)

CARLO (*rushing at him*). Have at you ! (*They come to grips.*)

(*The* CAPTAIN OF THE GUARD *comes in from the steps down* R., *a red-faced, fiercely-moustached fighter with an insolent blue eye, and all the impregnable vanity of the stupid man who has risen to authority. But instinctively a good soldier so long as he is not thinking ; and a humorist when he cannot be answered back.*)

CAPTAIN (R.C.). Now then! Now then! **Now then!** Now then! What's all this? What's all this?

(*The fighters draw apart from each other.* CARLO *up* C. TITUS *to* L.C.)

CARLO (*sulkily*). He insulted me.

CAPTAIN. *Insulted* you! By the Ivory Door and all the Little Devils! Insulted *you*! (*Looking him up and down.*) Five-and-thirty years have I been in His Majesty's Bodyguard, and never before have I heard of a Spearman being insulted! No, no, my lad, such compliments are not for a common soldier. You must wait until you are an officer for that.

CARLO (*meekly*). Yes, Captain. (*Crossing up* L. *for spear.*)

CAPTAIN. That's a good lad. (*Fiercely to* TITUS.) And what of you, boy?

TITUS (*taken aback*). He—he challenged me. I—I had to defend myself. He would have run me through.

CAPTAIN. And why not? Couldn't you have trusted your captain to have dealt justice on him afterwards?

TITUS. Yes, but—I—I didn't want to be run through.

CAPTAIN (*scornfully*). Didn't want! And are the fads of a common soldier to be allowed to interfere with the course of Military Justice? By the Ivory Door and all the Little Devils!

(*The Great Bell sounds.*)

Five-and-thirty years——

CARLO. Her Royal Highness!

(*He goes to the wicket-gate* C. *as the* SOLDIERS *come running out of the Guard Room.* TITUS *runs to* R.)

CAPTAIN. Fall in there!

CARLO (*turning at wicket-gate with a laugh*). A false alarm.

CAPTAIN (*to the men*). Fall out.

(*Exeunt* SOLDIERS L.)

What is it?

CARLO. A mumming-fellow. I have seen him in the tavern.

CAPTAIN. Come to give His Majesty sport, it may be. Has he any with him?

CARLO. No.

CAPTAIN. Let him in.

(CARLO *opens the gate and the* MUMMER *comes in. The* CAPTAIN *stands squarely in front of him down* L.C. CARLO *shuts the gate.*)

Well, friend, how is it with you?

MUMMER (*with a low bow*). His Majesty King Perivale beyond a doubt.

(CAPTAIN *about to twist his moustache.*)

CARLO. Ha-ha-ha !

(*He catches the* CARLO'S *eye, and stands hurriedly to attention.*)

CAPTAIN (*twisting his moustache*). A foolish mistake, friend. His Majesty is a younger man. (*Laughing.*)

TITUS (*laughing safely, the joke being the* CAPTAIN'S). Ha-ha-ha !

MUMMER (*laughing with them*). And, without doubt, plainer. I see it now. Your pardon for the error.

CAPTAIN (*nodding*). I like you, friend. There is that in your face which attracts me. You shall drink with me. (*Turning to table* L.)

MUMMER (*moving to* L.C.). It is most condescending of your lordship.

CAPTAIN. Say no more. (*Taking off his helmet.*) We have good wine in the buttery yonder. . . . I will await your return with the bottle. (*Sitting* L.C.)

MUMMER. Nay, but it is not thus that I offer hospitality to warriors. (*Clapping his hands in a lordly manner.*) Ho, there ! Wine ! (*Whisking out a bottle from the recesses of his clothing, and holding it out.*) Wine.

(*The* CAPTAIN *takes it.*)

CAPTAIN (*admiringly*). A pretty trick—(*drinks*)—and a pretty wine. Let me return your hospitality. (*Holding up his hand,* MUMMER *moving to him.*) I insist. It is a privilege to me to entertain genius. (*Putting down the bottle and clapping his hands.*) Ho, there ! Wine !

(*He looks anxiously at the back of the* MUMMER'S *cloak.* MUMMER looks round also.)

MUMMER (*shaking his head*). I have already drunk. Yet I thank you for your thought.

CAPTAIN. It is well. (*He applies himself to the bottle.*) We will sit down and consider the matter. (*Drinking again.*)

(*Giving* MUMMER *a stool* C. *and getting himself a stool from the table.* CARLO *moves down* L.C. *above table.*)

MUMMER. You have a wedding here ?

CAPTAIN. His Majesty's. We await the bride. (*Drinking.*)

MUMMER. I have seen no great company upon the road.

CAPTAIN. She comes alone. Such is the custom. One attends her to the gate.

MUMMER (*disappointed*). Ah ! (*Hopefully.*) Yet there will be feasting within the Castle ?

CAPTAIN. Without doubt. . . . And other entertainment. (*Drinking.*)

MUMMER (*anxiously*). You like the wine ?

CAPTAIN. Greatly.

MUMMER. I had wondered——

CAPTAIN. After another bottle (*squinting into bottle*) I shall be able to follow your argument.

MUMMER. It is an honour to converse with a mind so active as your lordship's. My little company sojourns below. At the time appointed——

CAPTAIN. If they are all as gifted as yourself—(*tapping the bottle*)—as I have seen you to be with mine own eyes—— (*Raising the bottle and drinking.*)

MUMMER. In the one particular, without doubt. They are well rehearsed.

CAPTAIN. I shall be glad to make their acquaintance.

MUMMER. In their performance before His Majesty, and his Queen, should they be so honoured, they will do you credit.

CAPTAIN. They shall not lack the opportunity.

MUMMER (*admiringly*). How delicately your lordship follows me.

(*There is a knock at the Great Gate.*)

CAPTAIN. And who might that be, disturbing honest men? Titus!

(TITUS *comes slowly across, but the* MUMMER, *eager to oblige, jumps to his feet.*)

MUMMER (*moving up* C.). Nay, friend, let me. (*Putting back stool, he goes to the wicket and comes back laughing.*)

CAPTAIN. Well?

MUMMER (*chuckling*). A wandering fellow who shared my breakfast. A pleasant melancholy fellow, yet a man of infinite jest. He would have it that he was a king. (*The* CAPTAIN *laughs. The* MUMMER *goes back to the wicket, and calls through it.*) Well met, Your Majesty!

(*He chuckles to himself and waits for the answer.*)

PERIVALE (*pleasantly*). What, is it the Emperor of China again?

MUMMER (*chuckling. To* CAPTAIN). You see? We have our little jest together. (*Crossing down* L.C.)

(TITUS *and* CARLO *and the* CAPTAIN *laugh.*)

CAPTAIN. I am a humorous man myself.

MUMMER. Who could doubt it of your lordship?

CAPTAIN. Titus, am I not a humorous man?

TITUS. Never was such before, Captain.

(PERIVALE *knocks.*)

CAPTAIN (*shouting humorously*). Your Majesty must needs wait! We entertain Emperors! (*With a laugh, then turning to the* MUMMER.) There! Was not that humorous?

MUMMER. Excellently diverting.

PERIVALE (*thundering*). Within there! Open!

(TITUS *and* CARLO *roar with laughter.*)

MUMMER (*proudly*). You mark the trick of voice ? *I* taught him that. He has a certain natural gift for it, but untrained. (*All laugh.*)

CAPTAIN. Well, let him in. He may have other tricks to show us. Tricks with bottles. (*Drinking again.*)

(CARLO *crosses up and opens the gate, and* PERIVALE *stands in the entrance, looking at them.*)

PERIVALE (*coldly, moving down* C. *Pause*). Well ?

CAPTAIN (*to his bottle*). It is well, friend. I am well, you are well, this bottle is well. It is well-nigh finished.

(TITUS *and* CARLO *laugh.*)

PERIVALE (*sternly, moving to* R.). Is this how you wait for Her Royal Highness ?

CAPTAIN. Her Royal Highness is well.

MUMMER (C., *admiringly, to* PERIVALE). Just a little more air—a little more—(*he makes a kingly gesture*)—but promising, very promising.

PERIVALE (*moving towards, impatiently*). Peace, fool, we are not mumming now.

CAPTAIN (*closing his eyes*). Peace. It is a blessed word.

PERIVALE (C., *in disgust*). Drunk !

CAPTAIN (*getting slowly to his feet*). Drunk ! By the Ivory Door and all the Little Devils, you dare to call me drunk ! (*He sees* PERIVALE *and starts back, rubbing his eyes and blinking. Sinking down again on stool.*) I am drunk ! Titus, tell him I've never been drunk before. Tell him I'm a humorous man by nature. (*Taking up bottle.*)

TITUS (*crossing down on his* L. *and patting* PERIVALE *on the shoulder*). Now, now, friend, be reasonable. We're all humorous men here, but a joke is only a joke so long as the Captain is making it. Yours has gone far enough. (*Stepping back to* L.C.) Tell us your business and begone about it.

PERIVALE (*controlling his temper and looking at them wonderingly, then taking a step to* TITUS). What's the matter with you all ? Don't you know who I am ?

CARLO. Neither know, nor care.

PERIVALE (*mildly*). I am the King.

MUMMER (*shaking his head*). No, no, all gone now. (*Mimicking him.*) " I am the King." Hopeless, hopeless !

PERIVALE (*thundering*). Fool ! I am the King !

MUMMER. Ah, that's better !

TITUS (*taking him to* R.). Now, now, I'm your friend. Take my advice and go home before there's trouble.

CAPTAIN. Drunk ! After one bottle ! (*Putting bottle to forehead.*)

PERIVALE (*bewildered*). What has happened? (*To* TITUS.) You are new to His Majesty's service. I do not remember your face. (*Moving up* R.C., *looking at* CARLO.) Yours, yes, but not your name. (*Dropping down* L.C.) But this—(*kicking a foot contemptuously at the* CAPTAIN)—old Bruno——

TITUS (*in awe to* CARLO, *crossing up* R.C.). Bruno! He calls a captain—Bruno!

CARLO (*tapping his head*). Mad.

(MUMMER *comes down on* L. *of the table.*)

CAPTAIN. Take him away. I don't like his face. Drunk!

TITUS (*coming down to* PERIVALE *at* L.C. *and pulling him over to* C., *earnestly*). Be reasonable, friend. If His Majesty had been outside the Castle, how should we not have known it? How was he to get through the gate, if no one opened to him? His Majesty is within, waiting for his bride. Be reasonable.

(PERIVALE *stands thinking. Then he smiles; frowns again; and finally, with another look round at them all, smiles to himself.*)

PERIVALE (*crossing to* R., *to himself*). The door was more magic than I thought.

TITUS (*taking a step up*). What's he saying?

CARLO (*without hope*). Mad!

PERIVALE (*mildly, moving up to* TITUS). Friend—for you seem to be friendly to me—could someone send for His Majesty's servant, that I might speak to him?

CAPTAIN (*sleepily*). We are all His Majesty's servants.

PERIVALE (*looking at him*). Clearly. (*To* TITUS.) But I meant his body-servant, Brand. It may be that——

(*But he is interrupted by a scream and the growing noise of some disturbance within the Castle—at first a confused uproar, in which no word can be identified.*)

CAPTAIN (*a man of war again; jumping to his feet and crossing up* L.). What's that? (*Roaring.*) To your posts, there. (*The soldiers come hurrying in from their quarters, three on either side of gates.*) Titus, Carlo, guard these two! This may be a plot. (*Roaring.*) Jump to it, my beauties!

(CARLO *to* MUMMER *and* TITUS *to* PERIVALE.)

(*Now voices are heard.* "The King!" "The King!" *And then a woman's voice,* "Dead!" SIMEON, JESSICA *and others appear for a moment at the Palace doors.*)

Fall in the Guard.

SIMEON. The King!

CAPTAIN (*sharply*). Well, what of the King?

JESSICA. Dead!

CAPTAIN. Dead?

JESSICA. And Her Royal Highness all but here!

CAPTAIN. How dead?

SIMEON. He went through the Ivory Door!

JESSICA. He's dead.

CAPTAIN (*nodding his head in awe*). He did so! In the name of the Door and all the Little Devils, why should he do that?

SIMEON. He found the key. He would go. Brand tried to stay him. He said he must *know* what was there.

CAPTAIN (*grimly*). And now he knows.

PERIVALE (*ironically*). And now he knows.

(*The* CAPTAIN *turns sharply to him.*)

CAPTAIN. Ah! . . . Ah! (*To* SIMEON.) Where is Brand?

SIMEON. With the Chancellor, Captain—acquainting him of the dreadful news.

CAPTAIN. Tell His Excellency that I have a prisoner here who can throw some light on the matter.

SIMEON. Yes, Captain.

(*Exeunt* SIMEON *and crowd, followed by* JESSICA *and the others.*)

CAPTAIN (*coming down to* PERIVALE *at* R.C.) And now, my friend, we come back to you.

PERIVALE (*leaving his guard, half-mockingly, half-regally*). We are delighted to give you audience.

MUMMER. But what—— The King is *dead*, they say? Who——

CAPTAIN (*thoughtfully*). And you. Now I wonder if *you* come into it. (*To* CARLO.) Here! Take the old man away, and keep him where I can lay my hand on him.

MUMMER (*indignantly*). *Old* man! (*To* CARLO.) Keep your hands off me! (*With dignity.*) I have played Kings in the presence of Kings.

CAPTAIN. Ay, there are too many who have played Kings. I do not like this playing of Kings. (*To* CARLO.) Take him off.

(*The* MUMMER *is pushed off, protesting.*)

PERIVALE. There is no harm in him.

CAPTAIN. I care not for him. (*Softly.*) But what of you, friend? (*Poking him in the chest with a finger.*) You come pat to the moment. The King is dead—and lo! In struts one, like to the King, who says he *is* the King! How came it that you *knew* the King was dead and could not give you the lie?

PERIVALE (*with a smile*). You are too subtle for me, Bruno.

CAPTAIN (*with a laugh*). Try again, Master King. It would not be difficult to learn my name.

PERIVALE. Yet the fact that I know it is hardly proof that I am not the King.

CAPTAIN (*poking him in the chest*). Pat to the moment.

PERIVALE (*brushing tunic*). Do you know, you are the only man who has ever done that to me ? I don't think I like it.

CAPTAIN. What if I say to you that you were lurking behind the Ivory Door when the King went through ? That it was you who killed him ?

PERIVALE (*contemptuously*). I thought they were Devils, not men, who waited behind the door.

CAPTAIN. And why should you not be one of them ?

PERIVALE. Looking like this ? Without horns and a tail ? Oh, come !

CAPTAIN. As you say. Looking like this. Taking on human shape. The shape of his late lamented Majesty.

PERIVALE (*ironically*). Oh, you do see a likeness ?

CAPTAIN (*grimly*). I do. That's what makes me suspicious.

(*The* CHANCELLOR *comes in from* R. *on to steps, followed respectfully by some of the people.*)

CAPTAIN. Hold him !

(*Soldiers surround* PERIVALE *and he is taken back up* R.)

CHANCELLOR. Alas ! Alas ! Woeful news ! His blessed Majesty dead—and on his marriage day ! But we must be calm. We must think what is best (*moving to* C.), what is safest. We must exercise our brains.

CAPTAIN (L., *coming to him*). You do the thinking, Excellency, and I will do the acting.

CHANCELLOR. Yes, yes, we must act. But first we must think . . . I warned him not to. I took that liberty. "Your Majesty," I said, "it is wiser, it is safer, to avert the eye—and the mind—from the unknown." I ventured to warn him. I said, "Your Majesty, be guided by me."

(BEPPO *enters.*)

Do not defy these evil spirits." Alas, alas !

BEPPO (*to his neighbour*). A bottomless pit a-full of devils. Didn't I say ?

CHANCELLOR. Alas, alas !

CAPTAIN (*impatiently*). Alas ! Yes. And now to deeds, Excellency.

CHANCELLOR (*petulantly, in a temper*). Deeds ! Would you have me tell you to go through the Ivory Door after His Majesty ?

ALL. No ! No !

CAPTAIN (*bravely*). An it were necessary, I would——

ALL. Bravo ! (*And murmurs.*)

CAPTAIN. Or send one of my gallant boys——

SIMEON. Oh !

CAPTAIN. —but it is not necessary, Excellency. We know the evil fate which has befallen His blessed Majesty.

CHANCELLOR. We know—(*timidly*)—and yet we do not know.

CAPTAIN. At least we have the man who slew him.

CHANCELLOR (*bewildered*). We have the man——l

ALL. Where? Where is he?

CAPTAIN. Bring forward the prisoner, Titus.

(TITUS *marches* PERIVALE *down two steps.*)

(*All crane and creep nearer.*)

CHANCELLOR (*amazed*). But—but——

PERIVALE (*to the* CHANCELLOR). As you said, Your Excellency, you warned me.

CHANCELLOR. But—but—who—what—— (*Turning to the* CAPTAIN.)

THORA (*happily, kneeling at his feet and turning to the crowd*). His Majesty! His Majesty is alive!

ALL. His Majesty!

(PERIVALE *takes a step towards them.*)

CHANCELLOR (*happily*). Your Majesty!

CAPTAIN. Hold him, Titus! (*They move back to* R.)

BEPPO. Who is it? Whc do they say it is?

ANTON. His Majesty!

CAPTAIN (*as the* CHANCELLOR *advances to* PERIVALE). Hold him, Titus.

(*Murmurs from the* CROWD.)

(*The* CHANCELLOR *stops.*)

BEPPO. But he's dead. He went through the Ivory Door. Wasn't I telling you?

ANTON. Yes, he's dead. That's what *I* say.

CHANCELLOR (*a little doubtfully*). But, Your Majesty—I understood—Brand said——

CAPTAIN (*with a loud, contemptuous laugh*). So he deceives *you*, too!

CHANCELLOR. Deceives me? But is it not—— (*Doubtfully again.*) Yet if His Majesty went through the Ivory Door——

SIMEON (*nervously*). No man can go through the Ivory Door and live.

(*There are murmurs of assent.*)

(*More confidently*). No man can go——

PERIVALE (*crossing to* C. *to* R., *firmly*). Your Excellency, it is my pleasure to give you some account of my movements—and with that the matter ends. I went through the Ivory Door, as Brand has said. I came out beyond the Castle Walls. I walked round to the Great Gate. I knocked, the gate was opened to me—and I found the Captain of my Bodyguard with his bottle.   The wine would seem to be at work on him still.   That is all.   (*Raising his voice.*) I thank you all, good people, for your concern for my safety.

ALL.   His Majesty is alive !

(*They cheer and advance towards him* o.)

CHANCELLOR (*holding out his hand, overjoyed*).   Your Majesty !

CAPTAIN (*to* TITUS).   Hold the prisoner !   (*To the* CROWD.) Back there !   (*Crossing to* o.   *To the* CHANCELLOR, *who moves to* L.C.)   Give me leave to speak, Your Excellency.   (*To the* PEOPLE.) Now listen !   I am a man of deeds, not words.   But His Excellency tells us that we must think.   Well, think then.   In all our history how many have passed through the Ivory Door ?   A many.

CROWD.   Yes !   Yes !

CAPTAIN.   How many have been seen again ?   Not one.

CROWD.   True, true.

CAPTAIN.   Which is more likely then : that this man is the King come scathless through perils which no other man has passed, or that he is an impostor ; himself perhaps one of those Devils, those evil spirits, which, as His Excellency has told us, and as we all know, lurk behind the door waiting for their victims ?   You may say, some of you, that you recognize your King.   I say that if a Devil cannot take on the shape of this or that man, a poor Devil he.

(CROWD *murmurs.*)

Of course he has the looks of the King !   Would you expect him to come with a hooked nose and a long beard, and whine " I am the King " ?

(*Laughter.*)

CHANCELLOR.   True. . . .   Yet he *may* be the King, even though he look like him.

THORA.   It *is* the King !

CAPTAIN.   Peace, woman, these are matters for men.   (*To the* CHANCELLOR.)   He may be the King.   Or he may not.   I say he is not.   There are ways of finding out.   I say no more.   (*He stands in front of the prisoner with folded arms.*)

(*The* CROWD *chatters while the* CHANCELLOR, *looking nervously at* PERIVALE *and away, ponders the question.*)

These are spoken simultaneously.

ANTON (*crossing down with* JESSICA *and* BEPPO).   No, it is not the King.   I see it now.   He is not even like the King.

JESSICA.   But, Anton, how *could* it be the King if he was changed into a Black Leopard ?

BEPPO (*gleefully*).   *Two* Kings I've a-seen vanish into the air.   Stephen was one, and here's another.   No other mortal man has seen what I've seen.   Two of 'em a-vanishing into nothingness.

THORA. It *is* the King. Didn't I speak to him, face to face?

(BRUNO *moves up* C.)

(ALL *stop talking.*)

CHANCELLOR. H'r'm! Yes—— Well—— We must proceed cautiously. As has been said, there are ways—an examination into the matter must be held—there are ways——

(*The Great Bell rings.*)

ALL. The Princess! The Princess!

CHANCELLOR (*upset*). The Princess! Yes, yes. This is very —— This is without precedent. The Princess! What are we to say to her? What are we to say?

CAPTAIN (*slapping his knee, coming down* C.). By the Ivory Door and all the Little Devils, *she* has come pat to the moment, too! Friends, here *is* your way!

CHANCELLOR. How—— What——

CAPTAIN. Can a woman be deceived in the face of the man she loves?

THORA (*eagerly, clapping her hands and moving forward*). Oh, well done, well done!

(CROWD *all shout*, " Well done! ")

CAPTAIN (*speaking, facing up stage with his back to audience*). We know how it is between His Majesty and Her Royal Highness. If he is an impostor, will she not know, however like he be to the King? If he is her lover, will she not know, however unkingly he be dressed?

ALL. Bravo!

CHANCELLOR. It is true. We see with our eyes only, but she will see with her heart. (*To* CARLO.) Let her in. (*To the people.*) Let her be the judge.

(PERIVALE *gives a loud, mocking laugh.*)

(*To the* SOLDIERS.) To your posts!

(SOLDIERS *form up on either side of gate* C.)

CAPTAIN. Silence! (*Turning to* PERIVALE.) Say one word to her before she speaks, and I will run you through myself, King or no King. (*Crossing to* R. *of* PERIVALE)

PERIVALE. Alas! I have no word left. (*With a sigh.*) We have talked the truth away.

CAPTAIN (*to* TITUS). Open there!

(ANTON *and* JESSICA *come forward and cross* L. *Two women cross* R. *and up stage.*)

CARLO (*at Gate*). Who comes ? (*He speaks in the voice of one using a ritual.*)

A MAN'S VOICE. Her Royal Highness Princess Lilia is come to His Majesty King Perivale.

CARLO. Withdraw, and let her be.

(*After a moment, there is a knocking at the Gate.*)

Who knocks ?

LILIA'S VOICE. Lilia is come to Perivale.

CARLO. Let her come.

(*A* SOLDIER *from* L. *crosses to* R. *of the Gate.*)

(*The Gate is thrown open by* CARLO *and* LILIA *comes in. The Gate is closed behind her, when she is standing* C.)

Her Royal Highness Princess Lilia is come home !

(*It is not the* LILIA *of the picture. That was a cold stately woman : this is a young impetuous girl. That was beautiful ; this has a wayward prettiness, no more. She waits, looking from one to the other of the faces round her, frightened at a silence almost breathless.*)

LILIA. Well ? I am come.

(*Still nobody says anything. Her eyes go slowly from one face to another. As she comes to* PERIVALE, *you can almost hear the people holding their breath. Her eyes rest on him with interest, but no more. They pass on to the next in the group ; and now it is as if all the company breathed again in one long expiration.*)

(*With a pretty dignity.*) Will no one take me to His Majesty ? (*She turns to* PERIVALE.) Will not you ?

(*Angry snarls from* CROWD.)

CAPTAIN (*in fierce satisfaction*). Ah !

(*There is a threatening murmur from the* CROWD.)

LILIA (*to* PERIVALE). What is it ? I am frightened.

PERIVALE (*comfortingly*). No, no, you are not frightened.

LILIA. Will you take me to His Majesty ?

THORA (*rushing forward and throwing herself kneeling at* LILIA'S *feet*). Oh, Your Royal Highness ! (*She crouches there, sobbing.*)

LILIA. What is it ? (*Stooping to* THORA.) What is it, child ? I don't understand.

PERIVALE. The story goes——

CAPTAIN (*pushing* PERIVALE *roughly back*). Enough ! Hold him, Titus ! Madam, this is our good Chancellor, who will tell you.

CHANCELLOR. H'r'm !

LILIA. Yes ?

CHANCELLOR (*moving up* O. *to her*). Alas, Your Royal Highness, you come upon us at a grievous moment. His Majesty—alas! alas!—I have no words——

LILIA (*anxiously*). Yes?

CAPTAIN (*bluntly*). His Majesty is dead, lady. There are no words to make it less than that.

LILIA. Dead!

CHANCELLOR. Alas, Your Royal Highness, it is indeed so.

CAPTAIN. Killed by a base villain.

PERIVALE. Or so 'tis said.

CAPTAIN. Silence!

LILIA (*looking at and taking a step to* PERIVALE). Who is this man?

CAPTAIN. The knave who killed him.

LILIA (*her eyes on* PERIVALE). Yet he has a gentle face. I would trust him.

PERIVALE. He would be proud of your trust.

TITUS. Enough!

CAPTAIN. His face lies. He is all one lie.

(LILIA, *still bewildered, looks from one to the other, and then down at* THORA.)

LILIA. Who is this?

A VOICE. Thora, Your Royal Highness.

ALL. Yes, yes, Thora.

THORA. I am Thora, madam. His Majesty said that I was to be your friend. That you would be lonely and that I was to be your friend.

LILIA. Now am I very lonely if His Majesty is dead. Stand with me, my friend. (*Raising her, taking* THORA'S *hand, and then turning to the* CHANCELLOR *with dignity.*) Your Excellency was to tell me. (*Crossing to the* L. *of* THORA.)

CHANCELLOR. Your Royal Highness. . . . His Majesty—There is in the Palace a door through which none may go, nor going, may return.

LILIA. I have heard of it, but doubted the tales I heard.

CHANCELLOR. Alas, madam, they are true. It is the doorway from this world. His Majesty went through—why, we know not, save that he would. He has gone from us. He can never come back.

(LILIA *turns to* THORA *questioningly.*)

THORA (*pausing*). It is true, madam. He is dead.

LILIA (*to* CAPTAIN). Then why do you say that this man killed him?

CAPTAIN (*pointing a finger at him*). As soon as he knows the King is truly dead, he comes pretending to be the King. How should he do that if he were not there to kill the King?

LILIA. Is he so like the King, then?

CAPTAIN. Like, as Your Royal Highness sees, and yet not like, as Your Royal Highness knows. A King is easily taken for granted, madam. He deceived some of us at first; but not me, and not Your Royal Highness, who loved him too.

(*Again* LILIA'S *eyes rest on* PERIVALE.)

LILIA (*dropping* THORA'S *hand and taking a step to* PERIVALE, *to herself*). Who loved him too! (*She looks round at them all, wondering.*)

CHANCELLOR. As we know, Your Royal Highness.

THORA (*breaking down again*). And now he is dead!

(LILIA *comforts her.*)

SIMEON (*to his neighbour*). Yes, we know now. He is dead.

ANTON (*carelessly*). I always said so. From the first.

LILIA (*to* CHANCELLOR). Where is this door?

(*All start.*)

(BRUNO *starts and clicks heels.*)

CHANCELLOR (*anxiously*). What is in Your Royal Highness' mind?

LILIA (*to* CAPTAIN). You loved him, you say. How is it that you have not followed him through the door?

ALL (*loudly*). No, no! It is death. Death!

LILIA (*to* CAPTAIN). You are afraid of Death?

CAPTAIN (*coolly*). No more afraid of it than I am anxious for it, madam.

LILIA. Yet you will not follow him?

CAPTAIN. I will not follow a dead man. . . . But I will take vengeance on the living, madam, and—(*he bows to her*) I will be a faithful servant to the living.

LILIA (*looking round at them*). You are all so sure of his death?

ALL (*loudly*). Yes, yes.

CHANCELLOR (*sadly*). It is certain, Your Royal Highness. None has ever come back. It was so that King Stephen perished. And many another.

LILIA (*wonderingly*). What waits there then?

CHANCELLOR (*shuddering*). Death, madam. What else we know not, save that there be evil spirits there.

CAPTAIN (*putting his hand on* PERIVALE'S *shoulder*). And that this is one of them.

LILIA (*with sudden determination*). Show me the door!

THORA. Madam! (*Jumping up.*)

LILIA (*freeing herself, facing up*). Show me the door! (*Looking round at them all.*) You cowards! To be afraid of a little door!

PERIVALE (*apologetically*). It is rather an odd little door.

Titus. Peace ! (*Pulling him back roughly.*)

Chancellor. Your Royal Highness ! Consider !

Lilia. I have considered.

Simeon (*coming forward with a nervous cough*). Your Majesty, Your Excellency (Bruno *grunts*), Excellencies all, have I Your Majesty's permission——?

Lilia. Yes ?

Simeon. Your Majesty——

All (*in a loud whisper*). Royal Highness.

Simeon. Your Royal Highness is a stranger, not yet of this country. It had occurred to me—I was saying—that the Devil's power over those who venture through his door might be—might be—— (*He looks inquiringly at* Anton.)

Anton. Local. Local. It may be, it may be.

Simeon. Local. Might not have effect over one coming from afar.

All. Well spoken ! Bravo !

A Woman's Voice. Let her go, Captain !

Chancellor (*to* Lilia). There may be truth in what he says.

Lilia (*to* Simeon). Thank you.

Simeon (*in confusion*). It had occurred to me—I just—— (*He subsides into the crowd, and finishes his sentence to his neighbours.*)

Captain (*shaking his head*). I doubt—I doubt—but if she is set on it——

Lilia (*with dignity*). I do as I please in this matter. (*To* Thora.) You will show me ?

Thora (*fearfully*). I will show you.

Lilia. Thank you, Thora. (*Crossing* c. *to the* Chancellor.) You will not hurt this man (*she indicates* Perivale) until I come back ?

Chancellor. We will wait, madam, until—— (*He hesitates.*)

Lilia (*with a smile*). Until I do *not* come back, you would say.

Captain. We will wait two hours, lady.

Lilia (*gravely*). Thank you. (*She turns* c., *looking at* Perivale.)

Perivale (*taking it from his pocket. Pause*). You will want the key, will you not ?

All. The key ! . . . Of course, the key ! . . . Where *was* the key ?

Perivale. You will want to take the key with you.

Chancellor. The key ! I had forgotten the key. (*To* Perivale, *surprised.*) You have the key ?

Captain (*with a contemptuous laugh*). Of course he has the key ! Is he not the Devil's doorkeeper ?

All. Of course !

(Lilia *puts out her hand for the key.*)

Perivale (*giving it to* Lilia). You will want to—take it with you.

LILIA (*nodding and taking the key*). I will take it with me.
PERIVALE (*with a nod and a smile*). We shall meet again.

(*She looks at him, seems to be about to speak, and then turns abruptly away.*)

LILIA. I am ready.

(THORA *leads the way into the Palace;* LILIA *follows. One by one the people, as if not wanting to go, but irresistibly drawn, fall in behind the* CHANCELLOR. *Only the* CAPTAIN, *the Soldiers and* PERIVALE *are left. But the desire to see what happens to* LILIA *is too much, even for the* CAPTAIN.)

CAPTAIN (*to* CARLO). Here! Hold this man with Titus. Has he arms?
TITUS (*taking* PERIVALE'S *dagger*). Not now, Captain.
CAPTAIN (*contemptuously*). Let him rest if he will, but keep near him.
TITUS. As you say, Captain.

(*Again the* CAPTAIN *wavers; and then, with a jerk of the head to the other soldiers—an invitation to them to follow him if they wish—he goes into the Palace. They follow eagerly.*)

(*With a hand on his shoulder, to* PERIVALE). I warned you.
PERIVALE. You warned me too. If you will give me room, I will meditate on my folly. (*He sits down on stool* L.C.)
TITUS (*to his comrade*). Give him room. (*Moving to* R.)

(*They move a little away from him.* PERIVALE *sits there, his chin on his hand, thinking. Suddenly he jumps to his feet with a shout.*)

PERIVALE. Of course! This is what happened to Stephen!

CURTAIN.

ACT III

Scene 1

The Throne Room of the Palace. The Captain, *walking up and down* r., *with many a puzzled glance at the Ivory Door, and the* Chancellor, *standing by* Perivale's *throne, with many a frightened glance away from the Ivory Door, are waiting.* . . . Soldiers *in attendance,* r., l. *and* c.

Captain. She will not come back.

Chancellor. We said two hours. It is not two hours.

Captain. She will not come back. They will take good care of that.

Chancellor (*quivering*). They?

Captain (r.c., *nodding twice at the door*). They.

(Soldiers *all turn and look at door.*)

Chancellor (*in distress*). I do not like it. (*Dropping down* l.) See what His Majesty has plunged us into! The door was locked. Why did he open it? You cannot open a door from one side only. He was for venturing into *their* world, and he has brought them into ours. I warned him.

Captain. It was not by *my* wish that Her Royal Highness went.

Chancellor. She would go, she would go—and it is not yet two hours. . . . (*Nervously.*) Did you—when she—before the door closed behind her—(*going to him*)—did you see anything?

(Soldiers *look at door again.*)

Captain (*looking at the door, hesitating*). N—no. (*Firmly.*) No!

Chancellor (*nodding*). That was what I saw. (*Crossing to throne.*)

(Soldiers *wince.*)

Captain (*loudly*). I saw nothing! (*Looking at door.*)

(Chancellor *sits on throne.*)

Chancellor (*hastily*). Nothing. Nothing. Indeed, my eyes were closed. I would not look.

(*They all look at door.*)

(*Pause.*)

50

CAPTAIN (*pulling himself together and going to* R.). We shall do no good by this. What of the man we have ?

CHANCELLOR. The King—the prisoner ?

CAPTAIN (C.). Yes. Shall we have him in ?

CHANCELLOR. It is not the two hours. We said we would——

CAPTAIN. We said we would do him no hurt. We can question him. That will not hurt him.

CHANCELLOR. No.

CAPTAIN (*to Soldier* R.). Bring him in.

(*The* SOLDIER *goes out* R.)

CHANCELLOR (*doubtfully*). You are certain ?

CAPTAIN. Of what ?

CHANCELLOR. If we did not know that he could not have come back——

CAPTAIN. The King ?

CHANCELLOR. He is very like.

CAPTAIN. And yet not like.

CHANCELLOR (*nodding*). It is strange, that. Sometimes I feel—— You knew him well ? As well as I ?

CAPTAIN. Did I not teach him as a boy ? Sword and dagger, bow or spear—was there ever such a pupil ?

CHANCELLOR. I too taught him. (*With a sigh.*) How quickly he passed beyond me !

CAPTAIN (*conventionally polite*). He had a good master, Excellency.

CHANCELLOR (*equally polite*). As I was about to say, Captain.

CAPTAIN (*conventionally modest*). It was a privilege to teach him. But, as you say, Excellency, he passed beyond us. (*To the foot of dais.*) We shall have no other King like him.

CHANCELLOR. Indeed, no.

(CARLO *and* TITUS *come in with* PERIVALE.)

CAPTAIN. Stand him there.

(*The positions are :*—PERIVALE R.C., TITUS *and* CARLO *on either side, two paces above him,* CAPTAIN *above dais* L.C., *and the* CHANCELLOR *seated on the throne.*)

You will question him, Excellency ?

PERIVALE (*anxiously*). Is it the two hours ?

CAPTAIN. What is that to you ?

PERIVALE. I am anxious for Her Royal Highness.

CAPTAIN (*with a sneer*). Perhaps you have reason to be.

PERIVALE (*gently*). I am beginning to have reason to be. (*To* CHANCELLOR.) Is it the two hours ? (*Leaning forward.*)

CHANCELLOR. Not yet.

PERIVALE (*relieved*). Ah !

CHANCELLOR. But we would ask you some questions.

(TITUS *and* CARLO *push him forward.*)

PERIVALE (*with a shrug*). You will not like my answers.

CHANCELLOR. Your name ?

PERIVALE. Perivale.

CHANCELLOR (*with dignity*). Your *real* name ?

PERIVALE. Perivale.

CAPTAIN. An obstinate fellow.

CHANCELLOR. You persist that you are the King ?

PERIVALE. That I was the King. Your Excellency seems to have succeeded me.

CAPTAIN. An insolent fellow.

(*The* CHANCELLOR *rises.*)

CHANCELLOR (*with dignity*). Believe me, young sir, if His Majesty were alive, he would be seated here, and I should kneel rejoicing at his feet.

PERIVALE. We will try the position, when you are ready.

CAPTAIN. You have your answers pat. Answer this.

(CHANCELLOR *sitting again.*)

If you are the King, why did Her Royal Highness not recognize you ?

PERIVALE. She had never seen me before.

CAPTAIN (*with a scornful laugh*). As we thought.

CHANCELLOR. You admit it ?

PERIVALE. She had never seen the King before.

CAPTAIN (*calmly*). That we know to be a lie.

CHANCELLOR (*with a knowing smile*). His Majesty and Her Royal Highness were well known——

PERIVALE. Legend !

CAPTAIN (*pointing off*). Fetch the girl Thora.

CHANCELLOR (*puzzled*). It was well known——

CAPTAIN. It *is* well known.

PERIVALE. Legend. A love-match. You liked it better that way. Indeed, it sounded well.

CHANCELLOR (*peevishly*). Legend—it is an easy thing to say. Indeed, it does sound well. We shall have one coming and saying, " I am the Chancellor." " Your pardon," they will reply, " I remember the Chancellor——" " Legend ! " " He was a big man." " Legend ! " " He could read and write." " All legend." Indeed, it sounds very well.

(*He is pleased with his exercise in irony, but* PERIVALE *has not been listening.*)

PERIVALE. Is it the two hours ? She should be here.

CHANCELLOR (*very sarcastic now*). For one who has never seen her you are very anxious.

PERIVALE. I have seen her now—and I am very anxious.

(*The* SOLDIER *comes back with* THORA.)

CAPTAIN. Ah! (*Taking* THORA *by the arm.*) Now, girl! I heard you talking.

(THORA *shrinks back.*)

There is nothing to fear. But His Excellency would hear too. You were to be maid to Her Royal Highness?

THORA (*up* C., *anxiously*). Yes!

CAPTAIN (*up* C. *on her* R., *with a look at* PERIVALE). When His Majesty told you of this, he went on to tell you of something else. What was it?

THORA. Do you mean of his love?

CAPTAIN. I am asking you.

THORA (*to* CHANCELLOR). He told me of his love for Her Royal Highness, of how he had met her in the Forest in her peasant dress (PERIVALE *is dumbfounded*), of—of their love for each other—ah, the poor lady! All that love could not keep him alive.

CHANCELLOR. He told you this himself, you say? Of how he had met her?

THORA (*moving a step to dais*). Yes, Your Excellency. He was kind and friendly. We talked of Her Royal Highness—always of her.

CAPTAIN. And he told you how it was between them? He himself told you?

THORA (*nodding*). He told me how it was. How they had met.

CAPTAIN (*dismissing her*). Good girl. (*He makes a sign to* Soldier.)

CHANCELLOR. Thank you. That is all. We wished to be sure of it.

THORA (*anxiously*). Her Royal Highness——? (*The* CHANCELLOR *shakes his head.*) (*With a sigh.*) I knew it. (*Curtseys to* CHANCELLOR *and goes out* R.)

CAPTAIN (C., *to* PERIVALE). Well?

CHANCELLOR. Do you still say "Legend"?

PERIVALE (*with a shrug*). I say nothing—save that I was once your King.

CAPTAIN. An obstinate fellow.

CHANCELLOR. You give us no proof.

CAPTAIN. He has given us enough. If he wants more, I will carve it on him with my sword.

CHANCELLOR (*eagerly*). Ah, now there! I will not judge any man hastily. But there is proof you can give us. His Majesty was a mighty swordsman. It was well known to us all that he could engage any three swordsmen in his army. Now if you——

PERIVALE (*scornfully*). Ha !

CAPTAIN (*up* L.C. *above* CHANCELLOR). He fears it ! I was sure ! He fears me alone, and His Majesty could engage three.

CHANCELLOR. In philosophy, again, knowledge of the stars, illuminated lettering, painting, use of the bow, our King was known to excel the most gifted of his subjects. If you could show us—— We will be patient. It shall be for you to choose what you will show us. Then can we judge fairly.

CAPTAIN (*taking out his sword*). Let him choose the sword, and I will give him judgement and sentence in one thrust.

PERIVALE (*sadly*). Was your King so gifted ?

CHANCELLOR (*eagerly*). He was a man above all men to be praised.

PERIVALE (*shaking his head*). He was a man above all men to be pitied.

CHANCELLOR. So, then you will show us——?

PERIVALE (*curtly*). I can show you nothing.

CHANCELLOR (*distressed*). You do not help us. I say " Here are facts to be proved or disproved." *Prove* that you are the King. Our King could do this or that. What can *you* do ?

PERIVALE (*angrily*). All that your King could do.

CHANCELLOR. Then will you not do it for proof to us ?

PERIVALE (*smiling sadly*). Alas, I am doing it.

CAPTAIN (*impatiently*). You give us words. You have no deeds to show us. Kingly deeds.

PERIVALE (*bitterly*). Kingly deeds ! They are not done by Kings. (*Sadly.*) I have no kingly deeds.

CHANCELLOR. Then how can you be the King ?

PERIVALE. You make me wonder.

CAPTAIN. Why waste more words on him ? A King ! He ! (*He jerks a contemptuous thumb at him.*)

PERIVALE (*indicating them with a finger*). A Captain, a Chancellor —we are a poor company, but it is the best that we can do.

(*There is a noise outside* R., *and* ANNA'S *voice is heard. The* GUARD *lower their spears in front of the entrance.*)

ANNA (*entering. The* CAPTAIN *motions to the guard to let her in. She knocks their spears up with her stick. The* CAPTAIN *moves down* C.). How dare you talk to me like that ? Don't you know who I am ? Trying to frighten me ! Have you no manners ? Ah, there you are, dearie ! They said you had run away and been killed. But I knew you would come back. Why, there's your sweetheart waiting for you ! (*Chuckling.*) It would be a funny thing if you had run away from her just as she was coming to your arms. " No, no," I said, " they've been waiting for this day—I won't say for kisses—they've been waiting for this day, and now——"

PERIVALE (*smilingly, shaking his head at her*). Oh, Anna !

ANNA. What is it, Your Majesty ?

CAPTAIN (*contemptuously*). That mad woman! (*Coming to* C.) Take her out, Titus!

(TITUS *moves down* R.)

ANNA. What mad woman? What's he talking about, dear? (*To* CAPTAIN.) Leave us. His Majesty and I would be alone.

PERIVALE (*with a look at* CAPTAIN *first*). I think, dear, if you would go with Titus——

ANNA (*looking at* TITUS). Go with Titus, yes. He's a handsome young man. Come along, dearie (*taking* TITUS *by the arm*), come with me, I'm not so old as I look.

CARLO. Ha-ha-ha!

(*The other* SOLDIERS *grin.*)

(CARLO *pulls himself together, and tries to look as if he hadn't.*)

CAPTAIN (*roaring*). Take that woman out!

TITUS. Come along! (*He marches her out firmly.*)

ANNA (*as she goes*). I don't do this for nothing, mind you.

(*Exeunt to* R.)

CHANCELLOR. Really, really!

PERIVALE (*looking after her*). She called me Your Majesty. I must have been right after all.

CAPTAIN (*contemptuously*). A mad woman!

CHANCELLOR. And not a very nice woman.

PERIVALE. Still, she recognized me.

CAPTAIN. Ha! If that is the best you can do——

PERIVALE. No, I can do better than that. (*Moving up* R.C.)

CHANCELLOR. Well?

PERIVALE. Will you not send for Brand, His Majesty's body-servant? Who should know His Majesty so well as he?

CAPTAIN. What need? *We* know.

CHANCELLOR (*judicially*). But if we know, Brand will know. As he says, Brand is most closely acquainted with His Majesty. It seems to me——

(TITUS *returns.*)

CAPTAIN (*to* SOLDIER). Bring in Brand.

(SOLDIER C. *goes out up* L.)

(CHANCELLOR *standing with foot on dais. The* CAPTAIN *is close to him.*)

What disturbs you, Excellency?

CHANCELLOR. Habit. (*Leaning forward.*) For years my voice has answered "Your Majesty" to the voice of another. Reason keeps telling me that I do not hear that voice now, but I find that Habit has already answered to it. It is disturbing.

(PERIVALE *wanders down* R.)

(BRAND *comes in from up* L.)

PERIVALE (*commandingly*). Brand !

BRAND (*bowing and moving to him*). Your Majesty !

PERIVALE (*smiling*). Thank you, Brand.

CAPTAIN (*coldly*). What is this, Brand ? This tale of the Ivory Door was a tale for children ? This is your King ?

BRAND (*awkwardly*). I—I—Your Excellency—I did but say "Your Majesty" without thinking. There is—Your Excellency sees for himself——

CHANCELLOR (*kindly*). I know, Brand. It has been on my tongue to say "Your Majesty" many times ; yet we have proof that this is not the King, but an impostor.

BRAND. For the moment it was as if His Majesty was alive again. . . . (*Remorsefully, kneeling to the* CHANCELLOR.) I should have stopped him. I tried to, but he *would* go through.

CHANCELLOR. There is no blame with you, Brand.

(BRAND *rises.*)

CAPTAIN (*impatiently*). There is no talk of blame. Only tell us. You say, and you have known him well, that this is *not* the King ?

PERIVALE (*to* CHANCELLOR). May I ask him ? (*With a smile.*) It seems to be my last chance.

CAPTAIN. Well, Brand ?

CHANCELLOR (*to* PERIVALE). Ask him.

PERIVALE (*slowly and carefully*). Brand.

(BRAND *moves to him at* R.C.)

I came this morning with you to the door. You carried the lantern. I bade you pull the curtains. You remember. You tried to stay me. You warned me that the others never came back ; you told me that I was *King* Perivale.

(CAPTAIN *on dais becoming angry during this speech.*)

You remember. I pushed you away, and said mockingly that you should hide yourself, lest the devils jumped out at you.

(CAPTAIN *turns to* CHANCELLOR *on dais.*)

You remember.

(BRAND *nods at each incident.*)

BRAND (*intent on* PERIVALE). I hid—but watched you go.

CAPTAIN. You mean you watched the King go ?

BRAND (*turning to him with a start*). I watched the King go.

PERIVALE (R.). You watched me go. There was nothing there, Brand. A long passage under the ground—twists and turns here and there—a scratch, a stumble, no more—no danger—nothing. I came out by the stream that runs beneath the walls into the Forest. I rested. I climbed back to the Castle Gate. . . . Brand. Look at me well. Am I the King? These others have tales of me. Heroic tales. An' I were the King, I could do this and that. You know me too well, Brand. Look at me. Tell me—for indeed I am beginning to doubt myself now—am I the King?

CAPTAIN (*stepping down from dais, to* c., *ironically*). Is he the King? Come, Brand, tell us. The tales of the Ivory Door that have been handed down to us these many years, they were but tales to frighten children. Our good King Stephen, he is still alive. We have been afraid of a shadow. There is nothing here behind the door, nothing that we do not know. Our wisest men have been as fools. They have told us childish stories. There are no devils in the world—only children. Come, Brand! Is it the King?

CHANCELLOR (*anxiously*). Look, Brand, and tell us. Is it the King?

(BRAND *approaches* PERIVALE, *and looks earnestly into his face.* PERIVALE *smiles back at him.* BRAND *gives an anxious, furtive glance at the others, looks at* PERIVALE *again, almost apologetically now, and drops his eyes.*)

BRAND. It is not the King.

CAPTAIN. Ah!

CHANCELLOR. You have known His Majesty for many years. Of all of us you have been the most intimate with him. You have seen this man and you say that it is not the King.

BRAND. It is not the King.

CAPTAIN. Ah! (*Crossing away to* L.)

PERIVALE (*sadly*). Oh, Brand! Is it indeed so?

BRAND (*muttering*). It is not the King.

(*He withdraws up* c.)

CAPTAIN. Is Your Excellency satisfied?

CHANCELLOR (*sitting, to* PERIVALE). And now what do you say?

PERIVALE (*sadly*). It seems that I am not the King. (*Moving to between* CARLO *and* TITUS *up* R.)

CHANCELLOR (*pause for* PERIVALE *to take up his position*). Then what are you? (*With dignity to the* CAPTAIN *who would interrupt.*) No, no, I will ask.

PERIVALE (*with a shrug*). For you, what you think me. I can be no other.

CHANCELLOR. An evil spirit?

PERIVALE (*with a smile*). A disembodied spirit.

CHANCELLOR. But you are not the King?

PERIVALE. How can I be?

CAPTAIN (*grimly*). At last! You have said it!

(The sound of voices off is heard. The CAPTAIN *puts his hand to his sword. But before he can draw it there is an interruption. A growing tumult without announces the return of* LILIA.)

VOICES. The Princess! The Princess!

PERIVALE. Ah!

CHANCELLOR (*joyfully*). What is this? Her Royal Highness returned to us?

CAPTAIN (*returning his sword*). Let us hear what news she brings us. (*With a sneer to* PERIVALE.) It seems that you and your kind had no power over *her.*

PERIVALE (*thoughtfully*). What *is* "my kind"? I seem no nearer finding out.

*(*LILIA *comes in from* R., *the* CROWD *at her heels.* SOLDIERS *with spears down keep back the crowd.*)

SIMEON (*for the tenth time*). What did I say? Wasn't I right? Coming from afar as she did——

*(*PERIVALE *comes down* R.C.)

CHANCELLOR (*rising*). Your Royal Highness! Is there—— Need I—— I have no words for my joy. (*Moving to* C.) Come!

(He makes to conduct her to the throne, but she waits opposite PERI-VALE, *and stands looking at him with a smile. Then she gives him a little nod of comradeship.*)

PERIVALE (*with a little laugh*). Ah!

LILIA (*crossing to* C. *between* PERIVALE *and the* CHANCELLOR). Now I understand. (*Nodding again, then placing her hand on the* CHANCELLOR'S.)

PERIVALE (*smiling*). I wondered if you would understand.

CHANCELLOR. Come, Your Royal Highness! (*Leading her to the throne. She sits.*)

A VOICE. What of His Majesty?

CAPTAIN. Ay, what of His Majesty?

CHANCELLOR (*bowing to her*). Your Royal Highness, have you news for us of His Majesty?

LILIA. I have news, yes.

CAPTAIN (*eagerly*). You found his body?

CHANCELLOR. Alive or dead, Your Royal Highness, alive or dead?

VOICES. What news, what news?

CAPTAIN. You have found his body, lady?

LILIA. I have found the King.

CHANCELLOR. But alive or dead?

CAPTAIN (*impatiently*). Dead, we know. You have found the King—where?

LILIA (*pointing in the direction of* PERIVALE). There!

CAPTAIN. But——

CHANCELLOR. Do you——

(*The* CROWD *looks round for* PERIVALE.)

VOICES. Where ? . . . What did she say ? . . . There's no King here.

CHANCELLOR. Do you mean——

LILIA (*rising and crossing down to* PERIVALE R.C. *and taking his hand*). Here !

CHANCELLOR. But——

VOICES. Oh !

CAPTAIN (*bluntly*). He is an impostor, lady. We have proved it.

LILIA. I think he is the King.

VOICES. The King is dead !

LILIA (*smiling*). No !

VOICES. He went through the Ivory Door. . . . He's dead.

BEPPO (*pushing forward*). What's she saying ? Did she find his body ?

CHANCELLOR (*distressed*). Your Royal Highness ! This is very —I find this very distressing. This man——

CAPTAIN. Man ? Devil more like.

BEPPO (*pointing at* PERIVALE). That's no mortal man. Don't I know ?

CHANCELLOR. Your Royal Highness, we have been making an examination in your absence. This—man or devil—I know not— but whatever he be, we have proved that he is not our King.

CAPTAIN. Enough ! He has admitted it.

VOICES. Kill him ! Kill him !

(*There is much enthusiasm.*)

A MAN. Long live Queen Lilia !

(*There is much less enthusiasm.*)

CAPTAIN (*roaring*). Silence there ! (*To* LILIA.) Lady, he has admitted that he is not the King.

LILIA (*to* PERIVALE *wonderingly, taking his hand*). Who are you then ?

PERIVALE (*standing hand in hand*). I am that Perivale who was betrothed to Lilia.

LILIA (*nodding*). I thought so. (*To the others at* R.) Yes, he's your King. (*They take a step back up* C.) If he denied it, it was because you would have it so.

VOICES. Who ? . . . What ? . . . What's she saying ? . . . The King's dead, isn't he ?

CAPTAIN (*impatiently*). Enough of this ! We know——

VOICES (*angrily*). Yes—we know—we know.

CHANCELLOR (*with firmness and dignity, holding up a hand*). Good people !

(There is silence.)

We must preserve our courtesy towards this dear lady ; who has come to us, a stranger, betrothed to our King ; who left us so fearlessly in search of our King ; who has returned to us so miraculously in place of our King. . . . Your Royal Highness, there is no one of us who may not be mistaken. It seems to us that in this matter Your Royal Highness must be mistaken. We ask ourselves—if I may venture to put our thoughts into words—we say to ourselves : If this is indeed our King, how comes it that the Princess Lilia did not recognize him two hours ago ?

LILIA *(releasing* PERIVALE'S *hand and taking a step forward).* I was a stranger. Your King and I had never met until two hours ago.

(There is a roar of laughter from the CROWD.*)*

(Indignantly). It is true !

(There is another shout of laughter.)

PERIVALE. It can never be true now.

LILIA *(turning to him).* Why do they not believe me ?

PERIVALE. They have their Legend—of this as of everything.

CHANCELLOR. Your Royal Highness—forgive them—but the truth is, they know. Your pretty secret was no secret to His Majesty's loving subjects. We——

CAPTAIN *(bluntly to* LILIA). Then you did not find His Majesty's body ?

LILIA *(angrily).* I don't understand. There is nothing to find behind the door. *(Turning and pointing to the door.)* There is nothing there, but a long and dusty road. *(They laugh at her again, but she goes on bravely.)*

(Angry whispers begin amongst the CROWD.*)*

So then I knew that, if the King had gone through the door, he would have come out safely as I did, and that this was your King.

CHANCELLOR *(puzzled).* Yet how can this be ? For we know——
(He looks at PERIVALE, *wondering.)*

(There is silence for a little. Then slowly, in whispers at first, from the edge of the CROWD, *the doubt begins to spread, from one to his neighbour, until someone voices it aloud, and all take up the cry—* " Is it the Princess ? ")*

CAPTAIN. By the Ivory Door and all the Little Devils. you have said it ! *(To the* CHANCELLOR.) This is not the Princess !

PERIVALE *(with a loud laugh).* Indeed a magic door !

(He has taken LILIA'S *hand as the murmurs of the* CROWD *grew. She turns to him now in wonder.)*

(*The* CAPTAIN *crosses to* CARLO *up* R.C. *and gives orders.* The CHAN-
CELLOR *sits on the throne.*)

LILIA. What does he mean?

PERIVALE (*bitterly*). It strips us bare, that door. We bring
nothing back.

LILIA (*with dignity*). We bring ourselves.

PERIVALE. But how little that is. (*With gentleness suddenly.*)
You mustn't be frightened.

LILIA (*proudly*). Did you think I was?

PERIVALE (*looking at her intently*). No, it is I who am frightened
for you.

(*The* CHANCELLOR *has been trying to sort out this new idea.* The
CROWD *discusses it.* The CAPTAIN *gives an order to* CARLO, *who
goes out.* The CROWD *angrily murmuring.*)

CHANCELLOR (*grappling with it*). But—but——

CAPTAIN (*coming back to him*). Why, man, it stands out as plain
as a rock. The Princess Lilia came to us. She did not recognize
this man because he was not the King. She goes through the door
to her death, as everyone else has done. An evil spirit takes her
place, passes itself off as the Princess, and hails her fellow-devil as
the King. (*Triumphantly.*) Why, did you not note how they
whispered and plotted with each other as she came in?

VOICES. Yes! Yes! They whispered to each other.

PERIVALE (*to himself*). What a delicate thing is Truth! How
easily it overbalances!

(CARLO *comes back with a cord in his hand.*)

CHANCELLOR (*after thought*). It explains. It explains. I see no
other way of it—yes, it explains.

CAPTAIN. Explains! What else can it be?

VOICES. Kill them! Kill them both!

CHANCELLOR (*rising and holding up his hand*). Nay, wait! We
must be sure first.

CAPTAIN (*to* CARLO). Bind them together.

(*Spoken during tying business*).
$\left\{\begin{array}{l}\text{CARLO. Did I not say this Princess} \\ \text{of yours was the Devil's Brat?} \\ \text{TITUS. But this is not the Princess!} \\ \text{CARLO. Well, but she is the Devil's} \\ \text{Brat, which is what I said.}\end{array}\right.$

(*They are tied, her left wrist to his right.*)

PERIVALE (*to* LILIA, *as they are bound*). This was to be our
marriage-day. Now we are indeed joined together.

LILIA (*bravely*). Till death?

PERIVALE. I do not know. There may be a way out.

VOICES. Kill them! Kill them!

CHANCELLOR (*to the people*). We must be sure first. But how can we be sure ? In the case of the one—(*indicating* PERIVALE)—there were many who knew the King well, and could bear testimony, but in the case of the other, who can be certain ?—for there were but a few minutes in which we saw the Princess Lilia. (*Bending forward and looking at her.*) Is it the Princess ?

SIMEON. If I may be permitted, Excellency, the Princess was a thought taller.

VOICES. Yes, yes, she was much taller.

SIMEON. I remember saying—(*to his neighbour*)—did I not say ? —Her Royal Highness is a tall lady. At least, I corrected myself, she is not short. Now this woman is short.

CAPTAIN. Much wickedness in a little body. Let us make an end of it.

CHANCELLOR. Stay ! . . . Did any other notice Her Royal Highness in particular ?

A VOICE. Her hair was darker.

CHANCELLOR (*doubtfully*). Was it ?

VOICES. Much darker.

CHANCELLOR. H'm ! (*But he is doubtful.*)

SIMEON. If I may be permitted, Excellency, there is a way.

CHANCELLOR. Well ?

SIMEON. The portrait of Her Royal Highness which the Princess Lilia presented to His Majesty. That would not lie.

PERIVALE (*with a loud mocking laugh*). True, that would not lie ! Is it not the work of the Court painter himself ?

CARLO (*shaking him roughly*). Wait till they speak to you.

VOICES. What did he say ?

CAPTAIN. Is Brand there ? . . . Fetch the picture. . . .

SIMEON. If she were to stand beneath the picture, Excellency——

CHANCELLOR. In good time, my friend. (*He looks suddenly at the door, and away again.*) We shall see to it that we know the truth. (*To the* CAPTAIN.) Did you—— (*He looks at the door and shivers nervously.*)

CAPTAIN. What is it, Excellency ?

CHANCELLOR (*to himself*). The door—I thought for a moment—— But 'twas nothing.

(*The* CAPTAIN *looks at door.*)

VOICES. The picture !

(BRAND *comes in with the picture to* C.)

CHANCELLOR (*moving down to* L.C.). Ah ! Now we shall see. Two of you——

CAPTAIN. Carlo, Titus ! Hold it up.

(*They hold it above* LILIA'S *head. So unlike her is it that the* CROWD *bursts into mocking laughter.*)

LILIA (*sadly*). She is more beautiful than I.

PERIVALE. I had not noticed it.

LILIA. Were you disappointed when you saw me?

PERIVALE (*smiling*). With the picture, yes.

CHANCELLOR. Yes, yes, we know the truth now.

CAPTAIN (R. *of the* CHANCELLOR, *hand to dagger*). Of course we know. And now that we know?

VOICES. Kill them! Kill them!

CHANCELLOR (*holding up a hand and crossing in front of* CAPTAIN). We must—we must consider—I—— (*He wheels round suddenly, pointing to the door.*) There! Did you not see it?

CAPTAIN. See what?

CHANCELLOR. The door!

VOICES. The door! The door! Look at the door!

CAPTAIN (*bravely*). What of the door?

CHANCELLOR. I thought for a moment—— Is it locked? Who has the key?

CAPTAIN. Ay, it is locked. (*Doubtfully.*) I—I suppose it is locked. Titus—see if it be locked.

TITUS (*protestingly*). Captain!

CAPTAIN (*fiercely*). What! You would——

TITUS (*hastily, moving up to door*). It *is* locked, Captain.

CAPTAIN. It is locked, Excellency.

CHANCELLOR. Ah! I thought—it seemed for a moment—but you say it is locked. Who has the key?

(*The* CAPTAIN *looks at him, puzzled.*)

BEPPO. What do they say?

SIMEON. The door. His Excellency thought that it was opening.

There is a shriek from a woman in the CROWD.)

ANTON. It did open. I saw it. Opened and then shut again.

VOICES. The door is opening! . . . They are coming for us. . . . They have come for their friends! . . . Save yourselves!

(*There is a rush from the* CROWD *down* R. *to escape.*)

CAPTAIN (*roaring*). Hold there, fools! (*Contemptuously.*) Well, let them go.

(*The* CROWD *exit followed by the* SOLDIERS.)

(*Only himself, the* CHANCELLOR, BRAND, *and the two prisoners, with* CARLO *and* TITUS *remain.*)

CHANCELLOR (*nervously*). I—I was asking: Who has the key?

TITUS (*producing it*). I have it, Excellency. Her Royal—the woman had it. I took it from her when we bound them together.

CHANCELLOR. Give it to me. (*He takes it.*)

CAPTAIN (*crossing* C., *in a loud cheerful voice*). Well, how shall it be? Hanging, stoning, burning—how does one kill devils?

(LILIA *clings to* PERIVALE.)

PERIVALE (*in a loud whisper*). Fear not! Look where the door opens again! (*Pointing to the door.*) They are coming for us!

(*The* CHANCELLOR *had moved up to the door, but on this business retreats back down* L. CARLO *and* TITUS *move back, spears ready.*)

CHANCELLOR (*testily to* CAPTAIN). You hear? You see what happens? This talk of yours, so loud, so boastful—I will not have it! You think only of the moment; you leave it to me to think of the future. It is not a question of killing this or that evil spirit, but of closing up the door by which they come into our world.

CAPTAIN (*sulkily*). The door *is* closed.

(CARLO *and* TITUS *creep backwards slowly down* R.)

CHANCELLOR (*in a sudden burst of irritation*). Was there ever anything so foolish as a soldier's mind? I speak not of this door or that door, but of the fact that the barrier between our world and theirs is down. It is our task to rebuild that barrier. Kill! Kill! That is a soldier's only remedy. One rebuilds nothing by killing.

CAPTAIN (*with a sneer*). Your Excellency is frightened.

CHANCELLOR. I *am* frightened, and I am not afraid to say so; and you are frightened, and you *are* afraid to say so. That is all that there is between us. But I will not talk of these things here. (*He looks nervously at the door again.*) It is unwise, it is unsafe. I will not stay here and talk openly of these things. (*He moves towards an inner apartment.*) Let us discuss these things secretly and soberly. Come with me! (*Moving up* L.)

CAPTAIN (*sulkily*). Well, have it your own way. (*To* CARLO *ana* TITUS.) Wait here with the prisoners.

CARLO (*protesting*). Captain! (*He looks fearfully at the door.*)

CAPTAIN (*in a fury*). By all the devils behind the door, can I not even command my own soldiers!

BRAND (*moving down three steps* C., *then looking round to* CAPTAIN). You can command them, Captain, but what good are they to you, if they run away at the first alarm? (*With a contemptuous jerk of the head at the prisoners.*) I will look after these. *I* am not afraid. (*Taking out his dagger.*) If their friends come for them, they come for their dead bodies.

CAPTAIN (*crossing and clapping* BRAND *on the back*). There's a brave boy! (*Contemptuously to the other two.*) Guard the outer door if you have that much courage, and see that none comes in.

CARLO (*sheepishly*). Yes, Captain.

(*He and* TITUS *go out* R.)

CHANCELLOR. They are in your safe keeping, Brand? (*Anxiously*). You understand, we have not yet decided——

BRAND. I understand, Excellency.

CHANCELLOR (*to* CAPTAIN). Then come! (*With a last glance at the door.*) Come!

CAPTAIN (*with a swagger, to show his courage*). I come!

(*They go out up* L. BRAND *follows to opening, sees them go, and comes quickly back to* PERIVALE, *and drops on one knee* C.)

BRAND. Your Majesty, forgive me!

PERIVALE. Why, Brand, how is this? I made sure I was an impostor.

BRAND. It was I who was the impostor, Your Majesty.

PERIVALE (*to* LILIA, *who turns to him*). My servant who did not know me at first.

BRAND. I knew Your Majesty. How could I not know you, who have been so close to you?

PERIVALE. Yet you denied me.

BRAND (*rising*). Your Majesty, what help would it have been if I had acknowledged you? Would they have believed me? They would have tied me up with you as one in the plot. How should they believe me, when they did not want to believe?

PERIVALE (*facing front*). You are right, Brand. They did not want to believe.

LILIA (*surprised, facing him*). Do they want to lose their King?

PERIVALE (*looking at her*). No. . . . But rather him than their Legend. This story of the Ivory Door, we have lived with it, it has been part of our lives, for how many hundreds of years? But I have been King for three years only. When I came safely through the door, I was telling each one of my people that he was a fool and a coward. A fool to believe, a coward to fear. Could I expect them to cry to the world: "We are fools and cowards! Long live His Majesty who has proved it to us!"

BRAND (*to* LILIA). We have been proud of our Legend, Your Royal Highness. It is our own; something which joins us together. We talk of it often. We tell each other stories. We could not lose it.

LILIA (*with a smile*). Your Chancellor seemed as if he would be glad to lose it.

PERIVALE. Not the Legend; only the reality. . . . Well Brand? What now?

BRAND (*quickly*). Your Majesty, I knew that some way would come, if I waited. I think it is come now. You see how it is with His Excellency. He is afraid of doing anything to you, afraid of doing nothing. (*Moving towards them.*) I will go in to him presently, and tell him that I heard evil spirits whispering behind the door of what they would do if harm came to you. He will be glad to let you go.

E

LILIA. Back through the door?

BRAND. Yes, lady. I do not know—it is a new life—you will not be King and Queen again. But it will be life. I can do no more.

LILIA (*with a sigh of happiness*). Is there anything more than—just life?

PERIVALE. Come with us, Brand.

BRAND. As Your Majesty's servant?

PERIVALE. As our friend.

BRAND (*shaking his head*). I like myself better as a servant, Your Majesty. And I have a fondness for Kings. You spoke of a cousin. I will seek him out.

PERIVALE. As you will.

BRAND. Here! Take this! (*He gives him a dagger.*) That is always a friend. (*Moving backwards, bowing to up* L.) Now I go with a tale to the Chancellor. Courage, lady. In a little while.

(*He hurries out, calling* " Excellency! Your Excellency! " *in tones of horror.*)

PERIVALE. Let us use our friend while we can. (*He cuts the cord that binds them.*) It has hurt you? (*He looks at her wrist.*)

LILIA. I have not minded it.

PERIVALE (*picking up the cord*). Perhaps I should not have cut it. It was our wedding-ring.

LILIA. Are we wedded?

PERIVALE. I am not sure. At one time there was talk of my marrying the Princess Lilia. The Princess Lilia was a cold, proud, beautiful lady. She would have made a cold, proud, beautiful Queen. (*Placing dagger in sheath and taking a step away to* R.) As I am no longer a king, I feel that I should give her the opportunity to withdraw, if she wishes it.

LILIA (C.). She wishes it—and withdraws. (*She curtseys—he bows.*)

PERIVALE. I thought she would. (*Crossing to her.*) That leaves me free to seek marriage elsewhere.

LILIA (*facing to front*). Have you chosen the lady whom you will now honour?

PERIVALE. I have no choice in the matter. Reasons of State demand that my dynasty be joined to hers. I have a dagger and a suit of clothes, and she has a suit of clothes. For the sake of these great possessions it is necessary that we wed.

LILIA. I do not like these State marriages.

PERIVALE (*gently*). We could throw away the dagger and make it a love match if you were willing.

LILIA (*looking at him and lowering her eyes*). I do not know much about love matches.

PERIVALE. I asked my father once, when I was a little boy, if you had to love people *tremendously* before you married them. He said, "Yes, you should." I think he was right, don't you?

LILIA (*shyly*). I don't think I know what "tremendously" means.

PERIVALE. It means many things; but chiefly, I think, it means that in all your thoughts and in all your acts, in every hope and in every fear, when you soar to the skies and when you fall to the earth—always—you are holding the other person's hand. (*He takes her* R. *hand in both of his.*)

LILIA (*wistfully*). It is a lovely thing for it to mean.

PERIVALE. I found that out when they tied my hand to yours, and we stood there waiting. I kept saying to myself, "To think that I might never have known about this!"

LILIA. It helped me, to hold your hand. I *was* frightened, you know.

PERIVALE. You were so brave that only I knew.

LILIA (*placing her* L. *hand on his*). You will hold my hand if we are to go through the door together?

PERIVALE. Yes.

LILIA. I am a little frightened still.

PERIVALE. There is nothing to fear. It is Life, not Death, which waits behind the door for us.

LILIA. But I am a little frightened—of Life.

A VOICE (*from outside, nervously*). Are you there?

PERIVALE. We are here, Your Excellency.

(*A hand comes through the curtain holding the key.*)

THE CHANCELLOR'S VOICE. We do not want you here. Alive or dead we do not want you.

(PERIVALE *turns to her. She smiles at him and nods.*)

PERIVALE. We will go. (*Crossing to curtains up* L. *and taking the key.*)

THE CHANCELLOR'S VOICE (*anxiously*). You will tell them that we did you no harm?

PERIVALE. I can bear witness that you did us no harm.

(*The* CHANCELLOR *is heard no more.* PERIVALE, *key in hand, goes to the door and opens it, and stands there for a moment, looking at* LILIA, *then comes down* C.)

LILIA (R.C., *wonderingly*). It is a strange door. Last time we went through as King and Queen and we came out as man and woman. This time we go through as man and woman, and we come out—how?

PERIVALE (C.). Perhaps as lovers, for that is again to be King and Queen.

LILIA (*looking at him gravely*). It may be so. I would be glad to let it be.

PERIVALE (*holding out his hand and taking her up to the open Ivory Door* C.).   Come !   Let us be part of the Legend !

(*The light fades out as they go up.*)

CURTAIN.

(*And of them we shall see no more.   Darkness falls on them, and they are gone.   But we have one glimpse into the future.   We do not see much ; no more, indeed, than a vignette of an old head and a young head ; but we know that once more Youth is asking eagerly, and Middle Age gravely telling, the truth about things.*)

SCENE 2

The CURTAIN *rises on the same scene.   The Ivory Door is closed.*

(*The* KING *is seated on the throne and the* PRINCE *is sitting on the* L. *arm.*)

PRINCE.   And was King Stephen the last to go through the door, Father ?

KING.   No, my son, there was King Perivale.   He went through the Ivory Door on the morning of his marriage, and was never seen again ; and after much fighting his cousin came to the throne.   That cousin was your great-grandfather.

PRINCE (*eagerly*).   Tell me about it !

KING.   He was a very brave man, King Perivale.   None was ever greater in courage and strength and wisdom.   He was to be married to the Princess Lilia, the most beautiful woman who ever lived, and on the very day on which she was to be Queen, it chanced that she found the key of the door.   And being a stranger to our country, and not knowing of the terrible things hid behind the door, she opened it and passed through.   The King's servant saw her and gave the alarm, but none dared to follow her, save only the King.   As soon as the news came to Perivale, he drew his sword and rushed after her, knowing that he was to die, yet content to die with the lady whom he loved.   The door closed behind him . . . and neither of them was ever seen again.

PRINCE (*looking up at the door and leaning back*).   What *does* happen to them, Father ?

KING.   Nobody knows, my son.   Some say that there is a bottomless pit into which they fall—some say that the Devil himself lies

in wait for them—but this only is certain, that, of all those who
venture through the door, none ever comes back. . . .

(And so the Legend goes on.)

(The spot light fades out.)

CURTAIN.

NOTE.—*The dressing of the* KING *and* PRINCE *in this last scene can be of the
period of Henry VIII.*

*The stage is in practical darkness, only the throne is lighted by the spot lime
from the* O.P. (R.) *perch.*

FURNITURE, PROPERTIES, ETC.

THE PROLOGUE

Throne and footstool on dais.
Hamlet type of stool up L.C.
Another down R.C.
A long seat, in front of the window up R.
Heavy tapestry curtains to the Ivory Door C.
Heavy tapestry curtains at openings up L. and down L.
Heavy tapestry curtains at opening down R.
Key and lock and trick lines to the Ivory Door, which opens on stage and closes
    again at cue.
Stage cloth to cover the whole of the stage.
There should be a step to the Ivory Door C.

ACT I

SCENE 1

The same as the Prologue.

SCENE 2

The same again.
Lantern for BRAND.
Daggers, spears, swords, etc.
Key for Ivory Door.

ACT II

SCENE 1

Front Scene.

Rostrum leading down from R.
Stone seat on bank set L. of C.
Bottle of wine and bundle of food, etc., for MUMMER.
Daggers for KING and MUMMER.

SCENE 2

The Courtyard of the Castle.

Large gate (C.).
Bell (deep toned, to ring off L.).
Table, 3 stools (down L.), mugs on table.
Stone bench (up L.).
Spears and daggers for soldiers.
Sword and dagger for CAPTAIN.
Bottle of wine for MUMMER.
Picture of the PRINCESS LILIA (with cover for same).
Small rope or twine to bind PERIVALE and PRINCESS LILIA
Stick for BEPPO.
Parchment for ROLLO.
There are steps up to the palace entrance down R.

ACT III

The same as Prologue and Act I.
The curtains have been removed from the Ivory Door.

LIGHTING PLOT

THE PROLOGUE

Deep ambers and reds from floats and battens.
Deep ambers on perches from R. and L.
Light amber spots on throne down L.
Two floods of light amber for throwing through large window up R.
At cue :—"I'm waiting for it to tell me."—All lights fade out to Black Out.
Light amber strips outside all openings, except the Ivory Door, which is perfectly dark.

ACT I

SCENE 1

Lights as before—FULL UP.
Light amber spots on Ivory Door.
At cue :—"You will not grieve for me."—All lights fade out to Black Out.
Pilot light on till warning.

SCENE 2

Set lighting to take up curtain.
The stage is practically dark.
A streak of light is coming through the curtains from window up R.; the amber floods have remained on.
At cue :—When BRAND *enters with lantern*—come up in the floats slightly.
   As he draws CURTAINS *bring on all*—LIGHTS FULL.
The room is flooded with light as before in Scene 1.
                    This remains till end of the Act.

ACT II

SCENE 1

Front Scene. Morning.

Ambers and pinks from foots and first batten.
Perches focus on bank and around.
Same at C. to L.
Lights fade out.
Curtain down *at cue :—The* MUMMER'S *exit.*
Pilot light.

SCENE 2

The Courtyard

Open on set lighting
Ambers and pinks and reds from floats and battens.
Deep ambers from perches.
Flood outside the Great Gate C.—light amber.
Amber strips at openings down R. and up L.
Spots to PERIVALE and PRINCESS LILIA.
                    This remains till end of the Act.

THE IVORY DOOR.

ACT III

Scene 1

All lights as in Prologue and Act I, Scene 1.
At cue :—" Let us be part of the Legend." (Bus.) *They move up to the Ivory Door, and as they pass through the door*—all lights fade out to Black Out.

CURTAIN.

Pilot light on till warning.

Scene 2

The stage is in practical darkness with the exception of the O.P. perches; flood with light ambers on to throne L.
At cue :—" That all those who venture through the door."—Spot lights fade out.

CURTAIN.

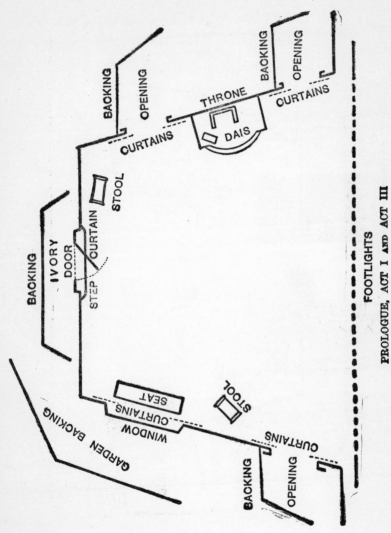

FOOTLIGHTS

PROLOGUE, ACT I AND ACT III

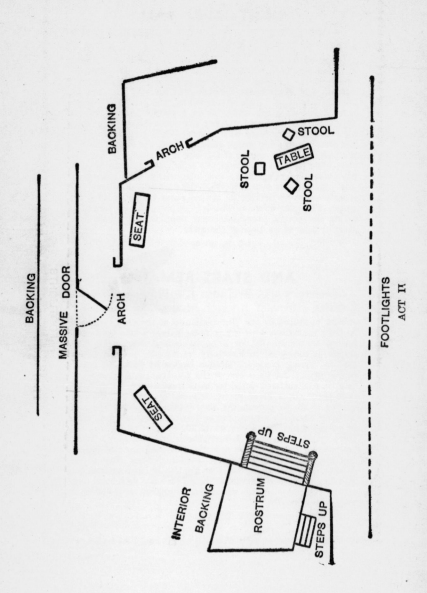

BACKING

BACKING

MASSIVE DOOR

ARCH

BACKING

ARCH

SEAT

STOOL

STOOL

TABLE

STOOL

SEAT

INTERIOR

BACKING

STEPS UP

ROSTRUM

STEPS UP

FOOTLIGHTS

ACT II

NIGHT MUST FALL

Melodrama. 3 acts. By Emlyn Williams. 4 males,
5 females. Interior. Modern costumes.

Produced in London and New York with Emlyn Williams
in the leading role. It is no secret that Danny, a bell hop who
arrives at the Bramson bungalow, has already murdered one
woman, and there is little doubt that he will soon murder
another—the aged owner of the house. He gradually insinu-
ates himself into her affections in a skilful manner, at the
same time managing to prevent her niece—who has guessed
his previous connections with murder—from giving him away.
For Dan is a dashing young assassin whom she firmly believes
she hates, but as a matter of fact she is fascinated by him beyond measure. Dan is a completely selfish, self-centered psycho-
path with no feelings and a vast imagination, who is perpetu-
ally acting for his own edification the part of a murderer, and
is only unhappy because he cannot share his secret with the
world. This play offers an excellent opportunity for some fine
acting and should prove extremely popular with Little Theatres because of its unusual character.

(Royalty, $25.00.) Price, 75 cents.

AND STARS REMAIN

Comedy. 3 acts. By Julius J. & Philip G. Epstein.
5 males, 4 females. Interior. Modern costumes.

First produced by the Theatre Guild at the Guild Theatre
in New York City. This is a comedy of how a family of Man-
hattan aristocrats, led by a pompous and dogmatic grandfather, is converted to humanity by a rude, young political
idealist. Young Frederick Holden begins by being an enemy
of the family, for he is one of the prosecuting attorneys who
has put a Trenchard in jail for bank fraudulence. Grandfather
Trenchard, in a fit of pique, sets out to ruin the political
careers of all the prosecutors involved in the case at which he
succeeds by tricky means, and as a reward becomes a director
of public works. But Frederick Holden's idealism has infected
the younger generation of Trenchards, and when grandfather
proposes to cut down the public works program and remove
the opportunity of making a livelihood from unfortunate
workers, the gay young folks in his family turn against him
and force a more charitable attitude. This is a delightful comedy with a current touch which should interest your audiences
more than usually.

(Royalty, $25.00.) Cloth, price $1.50.

THE GUARDSMAN

Comedy. 3 acts. By Franz Molnar. 4 males, 3 females. Interior. Modern costumes.

First done by Theatre Guild in New York with Lynn Fon-
tanne and Alfred Lunt. An actor and his actress wife, after
having been married for six months, have already come to
troubled ways. He is jealous and suspicious, and she has begun
to play Chopin again, music whose melancholy and autumnal
temper suits her mood and torments her husband. He has in-
vented a test of his wife's fidelity. He walks beneath her window dressed as a guardsman and comes to visit her. She pro-
tests that she loves her husband, but in the same breath she
leads the ardent young man on. The actor suddenly returns
from a supposed journey and seems to find his wife on the
point of a rendezvous. Behind the screen of his costume trunk
he puts on the costume of the guardsman and confronts her.
She has seen through his disguise from the start, she says, by
his kiss, and by his ardent eyes. They malign one another's
acting, they weep, and finally they make it all up. For advanced
casts. Especially recommended to Little Theatres and colleges.

(Royalty, $25.00.) Cloth, $2.00.

GOOD MORNING BILL

Farce. 3 acts. By P. G. Wodehouse. 4 males, 3 females. 2 interiors. Modern costumes.

First produced in London. Bill Paradene is spending a
holiday at Marvis Beach, Sussex, with Lottie. But Bill is getting bored, and Lottie, sensing this, has a fit of hysterics, and
Sally Smith, M.D., is called in to attend her. Sally turns out to
be the one and only whom Bill has fallen in love with on the
beach, but is terribly aloof with the unfortunate youth. He
pines so much for Sally that his stupid old uncle imagines
that he is missing Lottie, and sends for the girl, hoping that
the sight of such vulgar baggage under the ancestral roof will
cure him of his infatuation. Unknown to anybody, Bill has
telephoned for an urgent consultation with Sally, and many
complications arise when the two women meet late at night
with Bill. Everything turns out all right, however, when Sally,
who is determined not to marry a waster, discovers that Bill
runs a dairy farm, understands milk separation, and can recite
the names of innumerable bacilli. Sally's friendly understanding with the uncle on the variances of golf also helps to bring
things to a very satisfactory conclusion.

(Royalty, $25.00.) Price, 75 cents.